A Penguin Special
Acid Rain

Fred Pearce is the News Editor of *New Scientist*. He special-
izes in writing about water and has reported for *New Scientist* on the acid-rain debate for five years. He has written
one previous book: *Watershed*, which is a critical study of
the British water industry.

FRED PEARCE

Acid Rain

Penguin Books

Penguin Books Ltd, Harmondsworth, Middlesex, England
Viking Penguin Inc., 40 West 23rd Street, New York, New York 10010, U.S.A.
Penguin Books Australia Ltd, Ringwood, Victoria, Australia
Penguin Books Canada Limited, 2801 John Street, Markham, Ontario, Canada L3R 1B4
Penguin Books (N.Z.) Ltd, 182–190 Wairau Road, Auckland 10, New Zealand

First published 1987

Made and printed in Great Britain by
Richard Clay Ltd, Bungay, Suffolk
Typeset in 10/12 pt Plantin

Contents

Introduction

The skies above Europe are poisoned. Toxins are carried on the breezes from power stations and autobahns across the most polluted continent on earth. When the poison falls to the ground it chokes the pores of leaves on trees from the Alps to the Urals; it eats away at stone and brick, paper and rubber; it destroys soils and flows into rivers where it kills fish by disrupting the operation of their gills. It kills humans, too.

Acid rain is the phrase everybody uses to describe this poison. But rain is only part of the story. Acid mists and fogs are even more dangerous. London's most famous pea-souper, the smog of 1952, killed several thousand people. We now know that the water droplets in that fog were nearly as acid as the water in a car battery. Today, scientists are finding mists almost as acid on Scottish hillsides. Nowhere is safe.

The chimneys and exhaust pipes of Europe are creating an ever more complex cocktail of chemicals in the air over the continent. Some react with sunlight to form ozone, a chemical which damages trees and crops and irritates the human lung. Ozone also speeds up the conversion of other gases to acid rain. Countries such as Britain and West Germany have banished smoke. But clearer skies only make the cocktail more reactive and increase the threat from ozone and acid rain. The familiar heat haze seen on any sunny summer's day is made up of acid particles created by ozone.

All this should frighten us. Our forests and fish, cathedrals and crops, lichen and lungs – all are under attack. Today's air pollution is every bit as lethal as the black smogs it has replaced. And it is everywhere, from the most westerly shores of Ireland to the lakes of Scandinavia.

This book tells how, in little more than a decade, Europe's scientists have tracked down the ingredients of the cocktail above our heads, and developed the technology to clean up the pollution at source. They say they do not know all the answers yet but they are almost unanimous in calling for action now to stem the tide of pollution. They warn of increasingly dire consequences if their calls are not heeded. One by one, the governments of Europe are responding, promising cuts in emissions of the worst pollutants, of 30, 50 and even 60 per cent.

During September 1986, Britain finally and grudgingly shuffled into line. After a decade of fierce argument, the scientists at the Central Electricity Generating Board, whose power stations are responsible for two-thirds of Britain's acid emissions, conceded that those power stations were partly responsible for the disappearance of fish from Norwegian lakes.

Lord Marshall, the board's chairman, announced plans to spend £600 million over a decade, installing chemical equipment to clean up sulphur dioxide pollution at three of his twelve largest power stations. He would begin, he said, at Drax B, an extension to Europe's largest coal-fired power station at Drax in Yorkshire. The extension had only joined the national grid a few months before. The cost of adding the equipment now, rather than incorporating it into the original design, is around £40 million.

Marshall hoped by his announcement to cool the growing row that has soured relations between Britain and Norway over acid rain. It was made, in rather a rush, to coincide with a trip by the prime minister, Margaret Thatcher, to Norway. But she met angry demonstrators there all the same. And in Whitehall it swiftly emerged that the limited cleanup would barely reduce Britain's sulphur emissions. It would merely halt a rise in emissions predicted by the Department of Energy to last right to the end of the century. And, of course, it will do nothing to curb other pollutants, from car exhausts for instance, that are also poisoning and corroding the natural and man-made fabric of Europe.

1   A Pall over Europe

The Great London Smog

On 5 December 1952 a trick of the winter weather clamped a lid over London. For five days, the pollution belching from London's chimneys was held fast. Smoke and gas filled the capital, which became pitch black at noon. When the smog lifted, it left the mortuaries full, with 4,000 dead. It was the worst disaster from pollution ever recorded anywhere in the world. It is the start of the story of acid rain.

For Londoners, the worst week in the city's history began as just another smoky fog. They had grown used to them. And they had grown used to the grime in which they lived their lives. The city's buildings were black from decades of smoke. Deaths from bronchitis here and in other British cities were twenty times higher than in clean countries such as Norway and Sweden. Even as the fog blackened that week, as the water droplets in the fog mixed with the city's pollution to form a lethal acid mixture, nobody guessed at the human disaster that came with the blackness.

The Times recorded only one death from the smog: a bull, an Aberdeen Angus, wheezed and choked to death during the Royal Smithfield Show that week at Earl's Court. Another twelve coughing animals were put down.[1] The government's report on the disaster said afterwards: 'It must in truth be a supreme example of the way in which a metropolis of 8¼ million people can experience a disaster of this size without being conscious all the while of its occurrence.' It was not until the death certificates were assembled and analysed that the extent of the death toll emerged.[2]

On Saturday 6 December *The Times* reported: 'FOG

DELAYS AIR SERVICES. A pall of fog obscured the skies of London and some of the larger towns of England for most of yesterday.'[3] It was worst in the City, over the river from the new Bankside power station at Blackfriars. Much of west London was also blacked out.

On Sunday the 7th, an eerie black silence had fallen over London. It was the worst day of the smog. Ships on the river Thames came to a standstill. On the roads, 'the crews of the Automobile Association . . . found it almost impossible to locate members who telephoned for help. There was hardly a half-mile of road in the centre of London where visibility was more than five yards,' said *The Times*.[4] The streets were deserted 'except for an occasional convoy of buses crawling nose to tail back to their depots'. At Sadler's Wells, the opera *La Traviata* (whose heroine dies of consumption) was abandoned after the first act because the theatre had filled with smoke. In the East End, 'a walking escort of firemen guided motor pumps to a fire at a furniture manu-facturers'. Burglaries and muggings were rife – and the Aberdeen Angus died.

The great London smog was a single, vast acidic cloud, held down by a mass of warm air above. There was no wind to blow it away. The growing mass of black tarry smoke particles from the home fires and power stations provided the black nuclei on which more fog droplets formed. And the poisonous fumes of sulphur dioxide turned the droplets into a spray of concentrated sulphuric acid.

By Tuesday the 9th the smog extended for thirty kilometres in every direction from the centre of London. When breezes finally arrived later that day, the smog did not break up, but moved eastwards, slowly and intact. The giant black cloud, holding perhaps 500 tonnes of smoke, dawdled in the Thames estuary and passed over east Kent on the evening of the 10th, heading out to sea – no doubt helping to form one of the then-notorious fogs on the Dogger Bank in the North Sea.

The gentlemen of *The Times* wrote a stinging leader for their issue of Tuesday the 9th:

It is a common illusion of townsmen that their country cousins get off lightly in a fog ... The truth that fogs have taken to rubbing into us of late years is that they are not parasites of coal fires and other dirt-creating human agencies that they were once accused of being.

In this, its only comment at the time on the smog, the Thunderer was wholly wrong. Had those leader writers reached their country estates during the previous weekend, they would have found them largely fog-free. Since coal smoke was banished from central London, the number of days recorded as foggy by the London Weather Centre has fallen to less than a tenth that in the 1950s.

The bomb dropped on 18 December. The minister for health, Iain Macleod, rose in parliament to announce that, in the week of the smog, there had been two and a half times as many deaths in London and the surrounding metropolitan areas as in the same week of the previous year. There had been bad smogs before, notably in the 1890s. In the winter of 1948, around a thousand people had died in a pea-souper. But there had never been anything as bad as the 1952 smog. There were more deaths in London that week than at the height of the cholera epidemic of 1866.

Inner London fared worst. In the days before the smog, an average of five people died in Camberwell, a working-class surburb in south London. On 6 December there were twenty-one deaths and on 7 December, fifty died. During the five days of the smog, there were nine times the usual number of deaths in Deptford, seven times as many in Southall and five times as many in Finsbury and Chingford. There is a myth that the dead were either very old or very sick. Not so. The worst increase in rates of death occurred among those aged between forty-five and sixty-four.

Death certificates usually recorded the cause of death as a heart attack or bronchitis. Dr Bernard Lennox of the London Postgraduate Medical School described typical symptoms. The glands in the bronchial tubes that produced mucus became irritated, 'leading to the production of excessive quantities of mucin and ... inflammation of the large bronchi'. Most people died after choking on this mucus, either from a lack of oxygen or from a heart attack as they fought for breath – exactly as the Aberdeen Angus had died at the Smithfield Show.

Nobody could doubt that the smog was the cause of the deaths. But what was the lethal element in the smog. The smoke? The sulphur dioxide? Or something else? The smoke was the most visible pollutant and Lewisham's medical officer told the government's inquiry that 'the parts of the borough with the highest mortality were in proximity to sources of excessive smoke'. But smoke and sulphur dioxide gas went together. Most scientists of the day blamed the gas, but there have always been doubts. The official report noted that the deaths seemed to be concentrated in a ring round, but not including, central London. Boroughs such as Islington, Hackney, West Ham, Deptford and Wandsworth were hit worst, even though the smoke and gas was less intense than in central London.

The official report suggested that sulphuric acid, formed from sulphur dioxide, 'probably appreciably reinforced the harmful effects' of the other pollutants. Today, scientists think the acid was the main cause of the deaths.

Acidity is measured on a scale with its opposite, alkalinity. The scale, known as the pH scale, runs from 14 (extremely alkali) to 1 (extremely acid); 7 is neutral. Current estimates suggest that the London smog of 1952 had a pH of between 1.4 and 1.9, making it rather more acid than lemon juice.

The sulphuric acid was in a mass of tiny droplets, known as an aerosol, that hung in the air and could be breathed deep into lungs. The throat has a defensive mechanism against acid. It produces small amounts of ammonia to neutralize the acid and prevent it harming the sensitive lining of the lung. It seems that the London smog overwhelmed that defence in both humans and animals. The bull that died at the Smithfield Show, and the twelve others that were put down, turned out to be the ones whose straw bedding was changed most frequently. The dirtier straw of the survivors contained more faeces – which gave off ammonia, neutralizing the air in their pens. The 4,000 dead humans had no such protection.

Norway's Rain of Ashes

Henrik Ibsen was the first Norwegian to complain about black, sulphurous clouds blown across the North Sea from Britain to pollute his clean country. He wrote in one of his earlier plays, *Brand*, in 1866:

> Direr visions, worse foreboding
> Glare upon me through the gloom,
> Britain's smoke-cloud sinks corroding
> On the land in noisome fume,
> Smilches all its tender bloom
> All its gracious verdure dashes
> Sweeping low with breadth of bane
> Steeling sunlight from the plain
> Showering down like rain of ashes.

Oddly, many English editions of the play omit this passage. Most Norwegians believe Britain has been turning a similarly blind eye ever since.

The first scientific confirmation of Ibsen's observations came in 1881. W. C. Brogger, reported *'smudsig snefeld'* ('dirty snow') in Norway and said it came from Britain.[5] Thirty years later, the first mass deaths among salmon began in southernmost Norway: 1911 in the Kvina River, 1914 in the Mandal River. Professor K. Dahl, a leading Norwegian fish biologist, said that acid river water was to blame.[6] Norway's inspector for freshwater fisheries, S. E. Sunde, agreed. He wrote in 1936: 'All the Sorland [southern] rivers are more or less acid.' The Mandal and Kvina rivers were most acid. 'The Mandal, in particular, which previously was one of the country's best salmon rivers, having gradually almost entirely failed . . . Before the turn of the century there were fish in many trout waters in the uplands that are now empty of fish.'[7]

Sunde did not blame acid rain. He did not know about it. He believed that infiltration of acid from peat bogs in the 'uninhabited, uncultivated and desolate' uplands of southern Norway was to blame for the acid rivers. A series of warm winters had increased this infiltration, he said. 'There are therefore grounds for hoping that as soon as we get a period with cold winters again, the salmon will start to pick up.' He was wrong. There was no recovery.

The records of catches for the seven main rivers that drain the southernmost corner of Norway go back more than a century. They show that in 1900, anglers took 30,000 kilo-grams of salmon. The decline began sharply in 1910 and continued. Since 1970, no salmon have been taken. In the rest of Norway where, as Sunde recorded, acidity was much less, salmon catches have doubled.

The lakes, too, have turned acid. Fish started to go around 1920. By the 1950s, scientists began to report scores of mountain lakes that had lost their fish. The devastation accelerated in the 1970s and appears to continue today. Between 1978 and 1983, 30 per cent of the surviving brown trout in the lakes of southern Norway were lost, and 12 per cent of the perch. During this century, 67 per cent of the lakes with brown trout have lost their stocks. Today, fish are ailing or absent across twelve counties of southern Norway, an area of 33,000 square kilometres. In 1,700 lakes across 13,000 square kilometres (an area two-thirds the size of Wales) fish are virtually extinct.

It was a long time before Norwegian scientists first guessed that acid from the skies might be to blame for the loss of their fish. The suggestion was first made in the scientific literature in 1959.[8] Then in 1968, a Swede, Svante Oden, put all the links together and concluded that pollution from Britain and central Europe was responsible for the acid that was killing fish in both Sweden and Norway.[9]

The British government first formally admitted the link, after much soul-searching and a long rearguard action, on 19 March 1986. (Ironically, it was the same day that President Reagan admitted for the first time that US pollution was killing Canadian fish.)

Norway's lakes died as Britain built a new generation of coal-fired power stations. They are among the largest in the world and have tall chimneys to disperse the sulphur dioxide and nitrogen oxide emissions. The stations are concentrated

Salmon catch in rivers of Norway, 1900–73

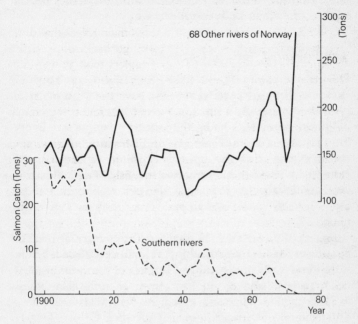

Only rivers hit by acid rain have lost their salmon.

in an arc from the river Trent in Nottinghamshire to the Aire valley in Yorkshire. The biggest concentration of power stations in Europe, and perhaps the world, is now on a twenty kilometre stretch of the Aire valley.

Three stations here – Drax, Eggborough and Ferrybridge – burn coal from the new Selby coalfield. They pump out a staggering 800,000 tonnes of gaseous pollutants a year, including 600,000 tonnes of sulphur dioxide. Between them, they generate a fifth of Britain's electricity and discharge almost a fifth of all Britain's sulphur emissions. It is as much as the combined national emissions of Norway, Portugal, Switzerland and Ireland. The final stage of this complex, the Drax B station, was completed in the middle of 1986. It was announced in late 1986 that Drax B will be fitted with cleanup equipment by the early 1990s. But Drax A and the other two stations will continue to pump out their pollution. This 'sulphur valley' will continue to be one of the largest sources of acid air pollution in the world.

The Poisoned Soils of Germany

During many winters, the fields, forests and autobahns of West Germany are covered in a light acid mist. You can taste it on the tongue. And smell it – a vast national reservoir of pollution mingling with the winter dampness. Every morning, 25 million people get into their cars, pull out the choke, swing on to the autobahn and top up the national exhaust by another billion cubic metres. When cold anti-cyclones invade from Siberia, the pollution does not go away. It hangs in the cold air and often seems thickest in the nation's forests.

During the two weeks I travelled the country at the beginning of March 1986, the thin, grey pall never lifted. There were smog alerts in the Ruhr valley, where the steel furnaces belch flames, smoke and gases over the Turkish 'guest workers' of Duisburg and Essen. And easterly winds bore sour, sulphurous fumes from neighbouring Czechoslovakia to trigger a second alert at the tiny border town of Hof, in northern Bavaria.

In Nuremberg, a hundred kilometres west of Hof, the city's air-pollution inspector told me how he sniffed the air in his garden at exactly 4 p.m. the previous Sunday and smelt 'cat's pee' for ten minutes, before it disappeared as abruptly as it arrived. 'It is the smell of Czechoslovakia,' he says. Next morning, in his office in Nuremberg, he found that automatic monitors had recorded a sudden tripling of sulphur dioxide in the city's air from 4.00 to 4.15 p.m.

West Germany gives as bad as it gets. It exports half a million tonnes of sulphur each year and imports the same. And there is always at least as much nitrogen dioxide in the air from its cars – the biggest cars, travelling faster and farther on the most extensive system of autobahns in Europe.

The country's post-war economic miracle has turned into

an ecological nightmare. The man who blew the whistle was Professor Bernhard Ulrich of Gottingen University. He is a small, smiling, elfin figure, with untamed greying hair, Hush Puppies and a polo-neck sweater. Hardly an archetypal German professor. He has spent twenty years measuring the chemistry of soils in the Solling forest, downwind of the Ruhr. In 1981, he appeared in the popular weekly magazine, *Der Spiegel*, telling a nation whose folklore is based on the forests, and whose trees cover a third of the land, that its forests were dying.[10] Decades of acid fallout from the German skies had turned soils throughout the country into reservoirs of acid. The acid was poisoning the trees and starving them of the chemicals that they need to live and grow. The roots were withering and soon the trees would die.

Ulrich claimed that the forest soils have been in decline since around 1880. Acid fallout today is around fifty times the natural rate he says: 'No forest ecosystem can withstand the present air pollution without serious damage.' In 1982 he predicted that,

after the next warm dry years, the forest damage will drastically increase. Dead forests, till now restricted to Czechoslovakia, Poland and East Germany, will become apparent also in West Germany, e.g., in the higher parts of the Harz plateau.[11]

Two warm, dry summers duly followed and by 1985 German foresters reported that 52 per cent of the nation's trees were in some way damaged – a fifth of them seriously.[12]

Today, there is one tree left alive on the peak of the Acker ridge in the Harz mountains. Six more stand marooned against the skyline, dead. The rest, thousands of them, are mere stumps poking out of the snow. Ulrich surveys the scene. He is subdued, but there is a gleam in his eye as he darts into the snow to point out the roots of a fallen tree. They demonstrate his explanation for this catastrophe. 'The roots should go down up to one metre, but look,' he says, 'they are all concentrated in the first twenty centimetres.' The finer roots are woody and deformed. They would not penetrate the acid subsoil, and could no longer find the nutrients necessary to sustain the life of the tree.

All along the ridge the story is the same. Signs ask visitors to take care of the trees. But the trees are gone. A hotel, the Hans Kuhnenburg, had built a platform above the trees so that tourists could survey the forest views from on high. 'Six years ago the trees were growing so well that they obscured the view and had to be cut back,' says Ulrich. 'Today those trees are dead.'

The Harz mountains lie midway between the Ruhr and an East German industrial zone around Leipzig. Whether the wind blows from the west or the east, the air is heavily polluted. Local politicians blame the federal government in Bonn for erecting tall chimneys to try and clear the worst Ruhr pollution from the streets of Essen and Duisburg. Lower Saxony's minister for federal affairs, Wilfred Hasselmann, says: 'When Willy Brandt declared that the skies over the Ruhr should be blue, he killed the Harz mountains.'

High on the Acker ridge, exposed to the biting easterly wind, a single sapling, its needles still green, pokes out of the snow. Ulrich says it cannot possibly survive. 'The soil here is so acid that it will not allow a root system to be established,' he says. The ridge is fit now only to become an acid bog.

More than two-thirds of the forest soils of northern Germany are acidified to the depth of a metre, at least, the level found by Ulrich in the Harz mountains. 'We have naturally acid heathlands in Germany,' he says, 'but in them the acid only goes down a little way. Here it is much worse, the whole root zone is acid. No new forest will grow.' Many more forests face the same fate as the Acker ridge. If Germany stopped producing pollution today, he says, it would still take the soil many decades, probably centuries, to revive.

What Goes Up Must Come Down

The clouds above Europe contain an extraordinary cocktail of pollutants. When the Scandinavians began complaining about the westerly winds raining British acid on to their mountains, they didn't realize the half of it. In the past decade, chemists all over the continent have revelled in compiling ever longer lists of chemical reactions taking place in plumes of power-station smoke, along cold fronts and warm fronts, in clouds, over land and sea and even over pig farms. The chairmen of organizations which have been shown to be responsible for pollution, such as Lord Marshall at the Central Electricity Generating Board in Britain, have paid their scientists handsomely to increase our knowledge of the complexities. The polluters hope that if they dig deep enough they will discover that their own pollution is doing somebody, somewhere, some good. It might neutralize acid rain, or fertilize trees or eat up some even-nastier poison.

They have had some successes. But the main messages from the chemists are still that what goes up must come down, and that two pollutants are quite likely to be three times as damaging as one. The gases that eat away at limestone, lichens and lungs in the city may reduce the barley harvest in the green belt, turn tree needles yellow in the forest in the next county, kill fish a thousand kilometres away and generate an acid haze in the Arctic.

The most important pollutants are sulphur dioxide and two oxides of nitric, nitrous oxide and nitrogen dioxide, which are often lumped together as nitrogen oxides. Both sulphur dioxide and nitrogen oxides are produced when coal and oil are burned. Both do serious damage in their own right and are converted in the atmosphere to the kind of strong acids that can produce dramatic reactions in a chemistry lab. Sulphur dioxide forms sulphuric acid, nitrogen oxides form nitric acid.

Historically, sulphur dioxide has been most important. It has gushed from millions of chimneys and, in harness with smoke, has been responsible for an appalling catalogue of damage to Britain and Britons in the two hundred years since the Industrial Revolution. It defiled the Ruhr industrial zone of West Germany and is doing similar damage today in parts of Eastern Europe. Once converted in clouds to sulphuric acid, it has also been the chief unnatural cause of death among Scandinavian fish. Today, most sulphur dioxide comes from power stations. They are responsible for almost 70 per cent of it in Britain. But, for all that, it is of slowly declining importance in Europe.

The rising stars of air pollution are the nitrogen oxides They come from power-station chimneys and car exhausts. The gas produces acid on a scale now approaching that of sulphur dioxide, and it is also a key ingredient in the formation of ozone, Europe's latest killer. Concentrations of nitrogen in the air have increased fourfold in Britain since the 1880s. In the richest parts of Europe, such as West Germany and Switzerland, where car ownership is highest, there is now more nitrogen pollution than sulphur pollution.

President Reagan spent his first term in the White House denying Canadian complaints that acid rain from the U S A was killing fish north of the forty-ninth parallel. If there was acid in the air, he said, it mostly came from volcanoes. Well, some sulphur dioxide does. But humans roughly double the amount of sulphur getting into the atmosphere. Coal and oil both contain up to 3 per cent sulphur, which is released when they are burned. Sea spray is the next most important source, followed by bacteria, plankton and rotting vegetation. In an average year, the world's volcanoes vent a little less sulphur than Britain's power stations. Overall, the coal and oil burned in power stations, boilers and oil refineries today send about 65 million tonnes of sulphur a year up the chimney. That is thirteen times more than in 1860 and twenty times more than volcanoes.

Europe is the most heavily industrialized, populated and polluted continent on earth. It produces almost half of the world's sulphur and nitrogen pollution. Over Europe, 85 per cent of the sulphur and nitrogen in the air comes from human activities. The belt of heaviest emissions stretches from the massed ranks of power stations beside the coalfields of central England, past the oil refineries of Rotterdam and the metal-bashing workshops of the Ruhr, to the giant Lenin steelworks at Cracow in Poland. A dense network of motorways covers the whole area. The air in this corridor is rich in sulphur and nitrogen gases, which turn to acid in clouds, or whenever they meet a film of water – on a church wall, or on the leaves of a tree. The rain, with an average pH of a little over 4, is almost ten times as acid as that west of Ireland or Portugal. (The pH scale is logarithmic. This means that rain with a pH of 4 is ten times more acid than rain with a pH of 5 and a tenth as acid as that with a pH of 3.)

Sulphur fallout over Europe

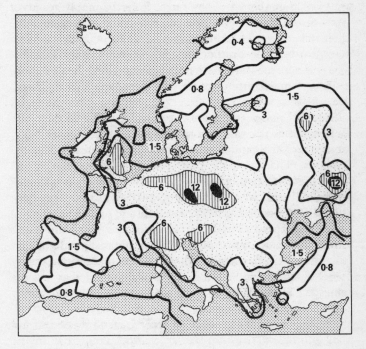

Total fallout of sulphur over Europe. Units are grams per square metre per year. Nitrogen shows a similar pattern.

Most of the gas falls locally in this polluted corridor, but some is borne upwards and can travel thousands of kilometres before falling in rain. Around 17 per cent of the acid that falls on Norway comes from Britain. About 20 per cent of that falling on Sweden comes from Eastern Europe. It can leap oceans, too. Perhaps 5 per cent of the acid falling in Europe has blown across the Atlantic from North America. And during most winters, a haze of pollutants from Europe and Soviet Asia settles over the Arctic. In Greenland, ice formed since the 1950s has been made acid by pollution.

Sulphur and nitrogen have the starring role in this book. But there are important parts for two other pollutants: hydrocarbons and ammonia. Dozens of different hydrocarbons are released into the air when coal and oil are burned or refined. They range from the highly reactive types to the most inert. The reactive ones, coming mainly from cars, solvents and oil refineries, are helping turn the air above Europe into a rather dangerous chemistry set. But the slow-acting hydrocarbons – from leaking North Sea gas, for instance – may turn out to be just as important in the long run.

Around London, there are two easily identified sources of hydrocarbons: the vast, amorphous mass of cars, centred on the heart of the capital, and a second, concentrated source down the Thames at the huge petrochemicals complex on Canvey Island. Taking Europe as a whole, the biggest single source of hydrocarbons is probably the complex of refineries around Rotterdam, in the Netherlands.

The importance of hydrocarbons is that they combine with nitrogen dioxide, especially in bright summer sunlight, to form ozone. Until a decade ago, nobody thought ozone was a problem in Europe. It killed trees and helped form nasty smogs in California, but Europe was not thought to be sunny enough to create much ozone. Then, in 1976, in the midst of one of the sunniest summers on record, massive concentrations of ozone were discovered across wide areas of Europe. Nowhere was safe. The west coast of Ireland suffered along with the home counties of England. Ozone, it seems, is even less of a respecter of national boundaries than acid rain. It invades high ground, where it clings to hillsides and escapes the mixing processes in air below. Ozone is especially persistent on the higher slopes of the Black Forest in Germany.

There is a lot of natural ozone around – notably in the ozone layer in the stratosphere. But there is growing evidence that much of the ozone found in air near the ground is a recent phenomenon and comes from human activities. Once again, the more scientists investigate, the more they realize how much man has contributed to the chemistry of modern air over Europe.

Ammonia comes from cow pats, pig slurry and human sewage. Millions of tonnes of it get into the air above Europe each year, where it combines with sulphur dioxide to form ammonium sulphate. Robert Angus Smith, the man who coined the phrase acid rain, knew about it in 1872. But nobody worried much until very recently, because the ammonia neutralizes acid rain. One study on farmland in northwest England found that 96 per cent of the sulphur in the air had been neutralized in this way. Acid rain turns alkaline in parts of rural Wales where lots of manure (both animal and human) is sprayed on to farmland. But there is a hitch. The ammonium sulphate damages foliage and, once in the soil, converts to acid again, while the ammonia turns to nitric acid. Ammonia, it now seems, could be a potent source of acid for soils.

The cocktail of pollutants above Europe is turning out to be very complex and very reactive. Short of putting a plug in every chimney and exhaust pipe, nobody can predict with certainty the effect of reducing one pollutant. Scientists enjoy this kind of complexity. It is part of their job. But they also have a duty to simplify a complex world – to make sense of the mass of data that they accumulate. Scientists at Britain's Institute of Terrestrial Ecology have fought through the complexities to divide north-west Europe into three pollution zones.[13]

The first zone is the old industrial corridor from England to Poland, where sulphur dioxide and, increasingly, nitrogen oxides predominate. In Eastern Europe, smoke is still a serious problem. But elsewhere it has been banished by cleaner boilers and power stations.

The second zone is the wet, Atlantic perimeter of the European continent, notably Scandinavia and Scotland. It is where the fish die. This zone has not suffered the worst ravages of industrial revolution. Until recently, the countryside gave every appearance of being unpolluted. The air itself is usually clean, but clouds coming from the industrial zones of Europe occasionally bring heavy loads of acid that may be dumped in rain or mists on to exposed mountainsides. The northern soils are thin and cannot neutralize the acid, which runs into rivers and lakes, killing fish.

The third zone is to the south of the industrial heartland of the continent. It includes the mountainous, forested areas of southern Germany, Austria, Switzerland and parts of Italy and France. These are the richest parts of Europe today, with less dirty industry emitting sulphur, but more cars and more nitrogen oxides and ozone in the air. Acid mists often shroud the mountains. Here, in the hazy, ozone-filled summer sunshine, we may be seeing the future of Europe's air pollution. The chemical mixture is at its most reactive. There are no black smogs to shut out the sun. The sun itself is now an important catalyst in the effervescing cocktail.

2 Corroding Gases

Industrial Revolution

Just before dawn on 20 February 1984, black snow fell on the Cairngorm mountains in north-east Scotland. Joe Porter from Grantown-on-Spey woke to find the ground black. 'I went out to walk my collie dog that morning first thing,' he says. 'The dog has white legs, but they came back black and with a greasy smell. It was a very noticeable band of black snow and it completely covered the ground.'

By chance, scientists from the University of East Anglia were in the area investigating the acidity of Scottish snow. Porter called them. They later described their findings in the journal *Nature*.[1] The event was, they claimed, 'the first documented case remote from major pollution sources of a distinctive, black, acid snowfall.'

At least twenty tonnes of black soot fell on the Cairngorms that night, says Trevor Davies from the university's School of Environmental Sciences. It formed a layer up to five centimetres thick and affected an area covering 200 square kilometres.

The scientists found large amounts of black carbon in the snow, along with lots of tiny glass-like spheres, the tell-tale signs of ash from coal burnt at high temperatures in power stations. The air that carried the black snow to the Cairngorms had passed across most of Britain that night, including the Trent valley and Yorkshire, where twelve of Britain's biggest coal-burning power stations are congregated. The amount of soot and ash dropped with the dawn snow would, the scientists concluded, require the entire emission for more than two hours from those twelve power stations. There can be little doubt that these stations are where the pollution came from. The event was remarkable, but not unique. Joe Porter says: 'This was the worst that I have seen, but each year we get some black snow. We got another layer that winter and another the following winter, too.'

Some people claim that the tall chimneys on modern power stations allow the soot to travel much further than before. But when Davies' colleague, Peter Brimblecombe, scoured the archives for reports of past falls of black snow and rain in north-east Scotland, he found them dating back to the 1860s. The Reverend James Rust was a weather-watching minister in Slains, a tiny hamlet on a headland near Peterhead, on the east coast of Scotland. He wrote a booklet on *The Scottish Black Rain Showers of the Years 1862 and 1863*. One January morning in 1862,

a large, dense, black, smoky, fearful-looking cloud, more resembling, excepting as to its immense size, the heavy dark smoke issuing from a steamer's funnel, that I had ever seen, came tumbling and driving along the sea in fearful majesty, and sent forth a shower of rain, a large proportion of the drops of which resembled dark or sooty water.

Next day, the lather in his shaving water 'curdled into a mottled black and uninviting compound. The water had an unpleasant sulphurous smell.' Rust said that black rain fell again in May 1862 and at the end of October the following year. Each time, Met Office records show that the air had blown across industrial areas of England. Rust wrote that he expected the black showers would 'in the end obtain world-wide fame'. In fact his booklet disappeared without trace until its discovery by Brimblecombe and his colleagues.

Sulphurous fumes and smoke have plagued the city-dwellers of Britain for centuries. The first attempt to ban coal in London came in 1273, and two special commissions examined the problem in the 1280s. By the mid seventeenth century it was widely believed that coal smoke was a killer. John Evelyn, a celebrated diarist of the day, blamed smoke when he wrote in a treatise called *Fumifugium*:[2] 'almost half of them that perish in London die of physical and pulmonic distempers ... the inhabitants are never free from coughs and importunate rheumatisms.' The smoke was also corroding iron and building stone and killing plants, he said. The smoke seemed to encourage fogs, and doctors blamed the spread of rickets in the capital on a lack of sunlight, due to smoke.

These were all very local phenomena. The real origin of acid rain was the Industrial Revolution in the north of Britain. Engels called Manchester 'the masterpiece of the Industrial Revolution'. Britain's first official air-pollution inspector worked there. His name was Robert Angus Smith – and he both invented the term acid rain and described most of its symptoms. He set up a network of rain collectors around Manchester and in 1851 he told the British Association for the Advancement of Science that 'all the rain was found to contain sulphuric acid in proportion as it approached the town'. In his classic work, *Air and Rain*, published in 1872,[3] he wrote: 'When the air has so much acid that two to three grains are found in a gallon of the rain-water, or forty parts in a million, there is no hope for vegetation ... galvanized iron is valueless ... stone and bricks of buildings crumble.'

In most towns and cities the pollution came from the traditional British open fire – an extraordinarily inefficient means of burning coal, but one to which the British were attached. In the 1930s, scientists estimated that 6 per cent of the coal in a domestic grate was not burned. Much of the rest went up the chimney to fall as soot, blackening the neighbourhood and providing abundant nuclei on which fog droplets could form. In 1913, a paper in the *Lancet* estimated that 76,000 tonnes of soot fell on London each year – 270 tonnes per square kilometre. Over the whole of Britain each year, the output of a million miners for three days went up chimneys unburned.

By contrast, most German houses were heated by closed stoves burning smoke-free coke. A team from Britain's Coal Smoke Abatement Society reported that large towns such as Dusseldorf were 'pleasant and agreeable places of residence ... even the richest citizens continued to live within the city boundaries, a practice which has long since been abandoned in British manufacturing towns.'[4]

As London grew, the smoke generated ever more fogs. They reached a peak with severe, smoke-infested fogs, which became known as smogs, in 1873, 1880, 1882 and 1891.[5] The average number of days when fog shrouded the river Thames at Greenwich rose from twenty in the 1840s to seventy in the 1890s. *The Times* described one smog in 1898: by ten o'clock in the morning 'it was too dark to permit the reading of letters; and, half an hour later, the darkness was comparable to a total eclipse of the sun.' The smog of 1880 killed about 1,200 people, a figure only exceeded by the 1952 killer.

Glasgow had a series of deadly smogs. So did Lancashire. But the unheralded pollution 'capital' of Britain may have been Stoke-on-Trent in the Midlands 'potteries'. The town was known locally as 'Smoke-on-Stench'. In the mid-1930s, while the average concentration of sulphur dioxide in London was less than 200 micrograms per cubic metre, the average in Stoke was 850 micrograms – a figure only reached in London during serious smogs.

By the second half of the nineteenth century, there was no doubt that Britain had the most polluted air in the world. Smoke from the big urban centres was becoming a source of long-distance pollution, with black showers travelling from the Cairngorms to Norway. Layers of soot formed in sediments on the bottom of Scottish lakes from about 1860. In 1914, during a debate on air pollution, the House of Lords heard about Pennine farms where haymakers 'often emerge from their labours in the condition of colliers'.[4]

The hills of the southern Pennines lie between the great conurbations around Manchester and Leeds. Vegetation in the hills has been devastated by the impact of air pollution. Dr John Lee from the Department of Botany at the University of Manchester has recently published a series of scientific papers demonstrating that, over the past hundred years or more, acid fallout has destroyed vast carpets of bog moss that once covered most of these flattened hilltops.

In the preceding 5,000 years, the remains of successive generations of bog moss had created the thick blanket of peat that still covers the hills. But sometime during the early decades of the Industrial Revolution, as pollution spread up the valleys on to the moorland, most of the moss died. The destruction was, says Lee, a 'drastic change' to Pennine vegetation. In many places the disappearance of the moss has left the peat exposed to severe soil erosion – especially in tourist areas such as Kinder Scout in the Derbyshire Peak District, where ramblers' boots finish the job.

Mosses live almost entirely on nutrient chemicals brought down by rain from the air. So they have been especially vulnerable to the poisonous compounds in the atmosphere. Even today's apparently cleaner air over the Pennines is too toxic for the moss. While smoke and gas levels are lower, the rain on the moors is more acid than thirty years ago, and the mists are more acid still.

Nitrogen oxides from car exhausts blow ever more freely across the moors, especially since the M62 motorway was carved through the hills from Manchester to Leeds. When Lee dug up bog moss from the Berwyn mountains in north Wales and planted it at Holm Moss, a moorland fastness above Manchester, the moss died – apparently gorged on nitrogen.[6] A similar fate would probably await other plants, such as the bog myrtle and sundew, which disappeared from the southern Pennines during the nineteenth century.

Trees have better defences against air pollution than moss. They take their sustenance from roots deep in the soil. But on the southern Pennines they too have suffered appallingly from the fallout of the industrial towns. Roger Lines from the Forestry Commission has investigated the history.[7] He found that 'attempts at afforestation on the more difficult sites during the last hundred years have met with little success ... In the 1930s the Forestry Commission planted several plots, but the trees grew slowly and losses were heavy.' Other trials in the 1950s were also 'highly unsuccessful'.

The southern Pennines, he says, 'receive pollution whichever way the wind blows. Pollution-laden winds are canalized into the main valleys which run through the Pennine ridge from east to west.' Invasions of soot helped give these hills more days of fog than anywhere else in Britain.

These fogs would have been extremely acid. Monitoring of air pollution by the Forestry Commission revealed that until recently more sulphur fell here than in many surrounding towns. 'The commonly assumed progressive decrease in pollution when moving away from city centres was not justified,' says Lines.

This pollution was killing the saplings planted by the Forestry Commission. Lines says: 'In the 1950s the smoke carried far into the country districts of the Pennines, coated the needles of conifers so thickly that it must have restricted photosynthesis, even if it did not actually block the leaves' pores.' Conifer trees, which kept their needles through the smog-ridden winter months, suffered worst. The retreat of the smoke and sulphur dioxide since the 1960s has helped the survival and growth of some species. But even today, says Lines, 'the range of species that can be grown successfully in the industrial Pennines is much smaller than on comparable sites elsewhere.'

The London smog of 1952 excited public demand for action to clean up the polluted air of Britain. Naturally, there were letters to *The Times*. Dame Caroline Haslett complained in laboured prose that 'an increasing layer of moist grime on a polished table protested eloquently that I was paying a heavy price to my neighbour's indulgence in "nutty slack". My all-electric house causes no nuisance to my fellow citizens of London.'[8] Morley Bell responded tartly: 'Those of us who live under the rain of grits from the Lots Road and Battersea power stations may ask ourselves whence she derives her satisfaction.'[9] Most power stations were in cities at this time, and many were extremely dirty. The answer, almost everybody agreed, was a ban on burning smoky coal in towns, and a new generation of power stations to provide 'clean' electricity. The power stations would be built away from the big cities, and would have the latest technology for cutting emissions of grit and soot.

The government dithered, however. Recently released Cabinet records show that Harold Macmillan, the minister for local government in 1953, told his colleagues: 'Today everybody expects the government to solve every problem.

It is a symptom of the Welfare State . . . For some reason or another "smog" has captured the imagination of the press and people.' He suggested that the government form a committee. 'We cannot do very much, but we can seem to be very busy – and that is half the battle nowadays.'[10]

Sir Hugh Beaver chaired the committee of inquiry.[11] He reported in November 1954: 'We wish to state our emphatic belief that air pollution on the scale with which we are familiar in this country today is a social and economic evil which should no longer be tolerated . . . We are convinced that given the will it can be prevented.' Ministers were unmoved, until a private members' bill forced them to draw up their own Clean Air Bill, which became law in 1956.

The Clean Air Act gave grants for anyone who agreed to convert to smokeless fuel, and gave local councils new powers to establish smokeless zones. Most of them took up their powers with relish. The effect was to hasten a switch in the nation's fuel consumption from coal to oil. Oil is not usually smoky, but it is sulphurous and as smoke levels declined, concentrations of sulphur dioxide continued to rise for a decade. It was only the fortuitous arrival of cheap North Sea gas, which is neither smoky nor sulphurous, that saved the day. The last killer smog in London was in 1962. In it, 750 people died.

Today, smoke levels in London are on average one-tenth those of thirty years ago, and sulphur dioxide levels are one-fifth.[12] Few of the chimneys that still fill London's skyline ever spew smoke. And the city's electricity comes from power stations outside the capital, along the Thames estuary. Central stations such as Battersea and Bankside are closed. Traffic, especially diesel-powered vehicles, is now the biggest source of smoke in the capital.

Similar improvements are found all over the country. But towns still without smokeless zones remain smoky. Stoke-on-Trent is probably still England's smokiest large town. Northern Ireland is the worst region. On winter days clouds of smoke still hang over many smaller towns on coalfields, where miners receive free handouts of coal.

By and large, the tall-chimneyed power stations do their

job of dispersing pollution and ending local 'blackspots'. But
occasionally the cloud does not disperse. Then it may ride
intact on the winds, and black snow may fall in the Cairngorms, or a Pennine village may be shrouded in a caustic
mist. Britain's largest power stations can each send a quarter
of a million tonnes of sulphur dioxide up their chimneys in a
year. And given the right atmospheric conditions, big cities
are still vulnerable to smog. On 30 November 1982, pollution
levels soared in London and officials were close to calling a
smog alert. In the winter of 1984–5, 'the taste of sulphur
dioxide was once again apparent on a number of occasions as
short-term levels rose above 1,000 micrograms per cubic
metre,' according to scientists from the Greater London
Council.[13] During these modern mini-smogs in the capital,
the wind is always from the east and the scientists concluded
in 1985 that 'several large power stations to the east of
London' were 'the most likely sources'.

Since the 1950s, the chemistry of Britain's polluted air has
changed drastically. The smoke has largely gone. Much more
sulphur is pumped into the air – but two-thirds of it comes
out of tall power station chimneys and more of it is converted
to sulphuric acid in rain. Rainfall all over Britain, even in
former 'smog holes', is more acid. The most acid rain falls in
south-east England, but the rainswept western mountains of
the Lake District, Galloway and the Scottish Highlands
receive more acid and sulphur fallout in total.[14]

And then came the car. There are 17 million cars in Britain
today. And as fast as sulphur dioxide has disappeared from
the cities' streets, nitrogen dioxide has replaced it. The European Community is setting limits for the concentration of the
gas allowed in urban air.

'London could well have difficulty in meeting the standard,' says Duncan Laxen from the now-defunct Greater
London Council's scientific services branch. 'The problem
will be greatest along busy roads.'[15]

One of the best-known results of the reduction in sulphur
dioxide levels in British cities has been the return of lichens.
Britain's climate makes it the best place in the world to
examine these extraordinary plants. There are more than

SO₂ in central London (micrograms per cubic metre)

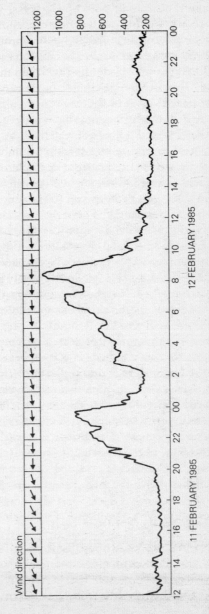

Easterly winds blowing up the Thames estuary can still bring high levels of sulphur dioxide to central London. Power stations along the estuary are a likely source of the pollution.

1,700 types known in Britain. They are extremely sensitive to sulphur dioxide and pollution has taken a heavy toll. There were 120 types of lichen recorded in Epping Forest, east of London, before 1865. Today, there are only twenty-eight.[16] Some recolonization has begun. A survey of London in 1980 found that several species had revived in the previous seven years.[17] But lichenologists are not dancing in the streets. They say that most of the 129 species lost to London since 1800 will not return unless levels of sulphur dioxide fall much further and it now seems that many species are almost as sensitive to acid rain as to sulphur dioxide.

Some lichens suffer because the surface on which they live turns acid. Oliver Gilbert has studied lichens in Monk Wood, high in the north Pennines on the border between Cumbria and Northumberland.[18] There the lungwort – an extremely sensitive lichen – lived happily on the barks of trees right through the Industrial Revolution. But as the rain has become more acid, so the bark of oak trees in the wood has acidified – from a pH of 5.2 in the late 1960s to 4.7 a decade later. In one stand, lichens were found on twenty oak trees in 1969, on five in 1978 and on none in 1984.

As some species of lichen return to cities, others are being lost in the countryside as the rain becomes more acid. The lungwort may be doomed. It is disappearing from the New Forest in Hampshire and from the once-clean valleys of west Wales. Meanwhile, species that do not like sulphur dioxide but shrug off acid rain are taking over. The beard lichen is proliferating. It was spotted in Leicestershire in 1984 for the first time since 1941. The British Lichen Society says: 'The invasion has been reported from Cheshire, Derbyshire, Tyneside and South Yorkshire. In some of these places, beard lichens have not been seen for 200 years.'

Smoke Signals from the East

Until the mid-1960s, Britain had the filthiest air in the world. Today, Eastern Europe has built up a commanding lead. The worst culprits are East Germany, Czechoslovakia, Poland and the Soviet Union.

But much depends on how you look at the statistics. After the USSR, Britain was until recently the biggest emitter of sulphur dioxide in Europe. Its two rivals are East Germanys and Italy. Look instead at the emission of sulphur dioxide per head of population and East Germany easily comes top, sending into the air 240 kilograms of sulphur dioxide per person per annum. It is followed by Czechoslovakia at 201 kilograms and Hungary at 153 kilograms. Britain comes eleventh at 83 kilograms and Poland is thirteenth at 76 kilograms.

Try the figures another way round. Look at which countries emit most sulphur dioxide per square kilometre of land. Here, again, East Germany is top at 35 tonnes per square kilometre. Next, at around 23 tonnes, come a clutch of countries, including Britain, Czechoslovakia and the Netherlands.

Which country dumps most sulphur dioxide on its neighbour? Here, Britain, surrounded by sea, figures nowhere. Most countries dump most of their 'exported' sulphur dioxide on the Soviet Union, as the prevailing westerly winds blow Europe's excess pollution towards the Asian steppes. Otherwise, the biggest outflows are both from East Germany – to Poland and to Czechoslovakia. The next biggest transfer is from Czechoslovakia to Poland.

There are few controls on air pollution in most of Eastern Europe. Most of the smoke and sulphur comes from fuel burned by heavy industry, rather than power stations. There is so much gas pollution in the air that nobody worries about acid rain or ozone. Eastern Europe contains three of the most polluted zones on earth. The first straddles the border between East Germany and Czechoslovakia, including the devastated Erzgebirge mountains. The second is the Upper Silesian coalfield of southern Poland. The third is around the Donbass coalfield in the Soviet Ukraine near the Black Sea. In each, the annual fallout of sulphur dioxide exceeds twelve grams per square metre over hundreds of square kilometres. This is twice anything seen in western Europe.

We know most about Poland because during the brief

liberalization, when the trade union Solidarity prospered in the early 1980s, a lot of information on the environment was published. The Polish Ecology Club for a while attracted a huge following and showed political muscle.

The pollution heartlands of East Europe

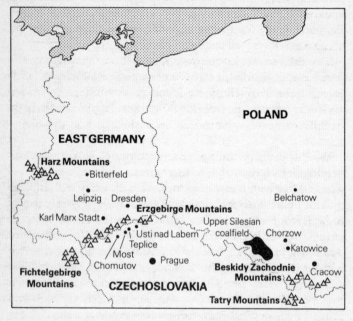

Poland's most damaged area is the Upper Silesian industrial region, around Katowice in the south of the country. Here coal mines, power stations, steel mills, metal smelters and chemical plants stand side by side in the blackened and acid air. They were built, with little regard for the environmental consequences, during three decades of fierce, post-war industrial development which turned Poland into one of the twelve most industrialized nations on earth. Between 1975 and 1980, while industrial production rose by 14 per cent, emissions of air pollution rose by 42 per cent.

Today, the small area around Katowice produces most of Poland's coal, 50 per cent of its steel, 30 per cent of its electricity – and 30 per cent of its pollution. Emissions of sulphur dioxide in Upper Silesia are five times greater, per square kilometre, than in the Ruhr, its nearest equivalent in western Europe. 'Katowice may have the worst pollution problem in the world,' says Professor Stefan Jarzebski, the head of the Institute of Environmental Engineering at the Polish Academy of Sciences.[19] In fact, the most concentrated source of pollution is probably the town of Chorzow, ten kilometres north of Katowice. According to official statistics, some 4,000 tonnes of sulphur dioxide and 900 tonnes of dust fall on each square kilometre of the town in a year. An hour's drive east is Cracow, an ancient town defiled by giant, polluting factories such as the Lenin steelworks. Some 1,700 tonnes of sulphur dioxide rain down on each square kilometre of the town every year.

One rare admission of the problems this kind of pollution causes the inhabitants of Cracow came in a broadcast on Radio Warsaw on 11 July 1984. It revealed that two of Cracow's largest housing estates, Wola Duchaka and Piaski Wielkie, had been blanketed in smog. 'The more sensitive inhabitants feel a lack of air because of vapours of unknown origin,' it said.[20] Twenty per cent of the Polish people live in areas where average amounts of sulphur dioxide in the air exceed the government's permitted levels (these limits are four times those set, for example, in the USA). In the past twenty years, the life expectancy of Polish men has fallen. And there has been an epidemic of respiratory diseases in industrial areas. Most people believe the cause is air pollution. Oxygen deficiency, a leading killer in the London smog of 1952, is said to be the prime cause of death among Polish babies who reach the age of one month or more.

The pollution is eating away at the thirteenth-century centre of Cracow. The average amount of sunshine in the city has fallen from almost five hours each day in 1945 to around three hours today.[21]

Just as Britain's capitalist Industrial Revolution destroyed the prospects for trees in the Pennines, so Poland's industrial revolution is destroying that country's forests. The government says that 6 per cent of Poland's trees are seriously damaged by direct attack from sulphur dioxide – double the figure for 1976. South of Katowice, in the Beskidy Zachodnie mountains, conifer forests covering 2,000 square kilometres (the size of Britain's Lake District) are dead or dying. Over the border, the Czechs report serious damage to trees in their Tatry mountains. Tourists are deserting the mountains, which were once one of Czechoslovakia's best-loved holiday areas.[22]

Stories about damage to crops and buildings from smoke and acid abound in Poland. Pollution is said to have corroded the railway tracks around Katowice so that a speed limit of forty kilometres per hour had to be enforced.[19] But Polish railways are in a dreadful state of disrepair, so the role of pollution is not clear. Two separate studies in Poland have concluded that the cost to the nation from corrosion and damage to crops and forests amounts to between 6 and 10 per cent of the country's industrial output.[20] So the nation's economic planners may one day regret their latest plan to open up reserves of highly sulphurous brown coal. The coal will form the basis for a new industrial region in the centre of the country, halfway between Katowice and Warsaw. The Belchatow industrial region is expected to produce around one million tonnes of sulphur dioxide a year. This will add more than a third to the current national output of 2.75 million tonnes.[23]

In 1981, as the Polish environment movement flowered, the Czech government asked its Academy of Sciences to write a report on the state of the environment in that country. Late in 1983, the human rights organization, Charter 77, got hold of a copy and smuggled it to the west, where it appeared in an *émigré* magazine.[24]

Czechoslovakia, like its neighbours, underwent breakneck industrialization, beginning in the 1950s. The fuel for the industrial drive was brown coal, mined in the far north-west of the country, between Prague and the border with East Germany. Here, the Bohemian towns of Usti nad Labem, Chomutov, Most and Teplice, huddled along fifty kilometres of the Ohre river valley, form one of the ugliest and dirtiest urban areas in central Europe. The Czech scientists identified

Most as the worst of them all. Many foreign visitors say Usti is worse.

Brown coal does not contain a high percentage of sulphur, but it does not contain much carbon, either. Half of it is water and huge amounts have to be burned to create enough energy for the giant factories of the area, such as the V. I. Lenin steel works, which manufactures the nation's railway engines.

One of Czechoslovakia's main exports is matches. They are perhaps the only things regularly bought by most western Europeans that are 'Made in Czechoslovakia'. So the claim by Czech scientists that pollution could, by the end of the century, severely damage half the nation's woodlands needs to be taken seriously by the country's economic planners. Nearly a third of the trees in the west of the country have been damaged by sulphur dioxide. The Czech national forestry service is replacing vulnerable conifers with deciduous trees which it hopes can survive. The leaves of deciduous trees are shed every year, giving the tree a greater chance to shrug off the pollution – at any rate until the soils turn acid. But in the Erzgebirge mountains, nearest to the industrial towns, it is too late. Vast areas of dead and dying trees have been removed. The people who once tended the forests have left and the winds blow the pollutions across a deserted landscape and over the borders into East and West Germany.

The economic consequences of this profligacy in pollution is put at a billion pounds a year by the Academy of Sciences. In late 1985, ministers in Czechoslovakia declared northern Bohemia an ecological disaster area and announced plans to spend seven billion pounds in the next fifteen years to clear up pollution of air and water.

East Germany is the most heavily industrialized country in the Eastern bloc. It is also the world's biggest producer of brown coal and, for its size and population, the biggest source of sulphur dioxide. Between 1980 and 1985, the country's emissions rose by more than 10 per cent, to five million tonnes per year. Its emissions now exceed those of Britain, a country more than double the size.

In 1984, the United Nations reported that 12 per cent of East Germany's forests were badly damaged by pollution: this was the worst in Europe.[25] The government replied that the claim was 'pure invention'. But at about the same time, ministers went to Prague for a joint meeting with Czechoslovakia to discuss ways of saving the Erzgebirge mountains along their common border.

Most of East Germany's formidable output of pollution comes from the south, around cities such as Leipzig, Dresden, Karl Marx Stadt and Bitterfeld (which visitors say is the most polluted). The country's largest power station, at Boxberg, close to the Polish border, discharges half a million tonnes of sulphur dioxide every year, more even than Drax in Britain.

Throughout this area, damage to trees is widespread. It stretches from the West German border to the Polish frontier and is worst in the highlands, such as the Harz mountains, the Fichtelgebirge and the Erzgebirge – where it often meets pollution from Most and its Czech neighbours coming the other way.

Information on air pollution and its effects in other East European countries is sketchy. The Romanian delegation to a conference on acid rain in 1984 said that 2,000 square kilometres of its country's forests had been damaged by pollution. Similar estimates come from Yugoslavia, where pollution is worst in the north, around Trieste and Zagreb.

In 1985, an agricultural commission in Hungary reported that Czechoslovakia was the main source of its sulphur pollution. Deciduous trees in north-east Hungary had been dying since about 1980. In this area pollution from southern Poland and the Soviet Union could be an important factor. According to Rezso Baross, a Hungarian researcher, damage is worst among holm oak trees, especially in the plains bordering the Soviet Union.

The Soviet Union's wide open spaces mean that away from the main industrial centres the fallout from pollution is much lower than elsewhere in Eastern Europe. But the Soviet Union's returns to the European monitoring programme identify four large centres of pollution. Three are around

Leningrad, Moscow and Kiev. The fourth, with much higher concentrations, is the industrial area of the east Ukraine known as the Donets-Dnepr economic región. The area, based on the Donbass coalfield, produces a third of all the Soviet Union's brown coal, half of its iron ore and a third of its steel. The Donbass has as much sulphur in the air as southern Poland. In 1979, a former Soviet official (known by the pseudonym Boris Komarov) published a book called *The Destruction of Nature in the Soviet Union*. He identified the people of Krivoi Rog, where huge iron-ore deposits support a large iron and steel works, as enduring some of the worst pollution from sulphur dioxide in the country.[26]

Lungs Full of Poison

They shut the schools in the Ruhr valley one Friday in January 1985. They closed factories, and put barriers across the roads to keep motorists out of the towns. A dense, cold smog had swept across central Europe from Poland and Czechoslovakia, to settle most heavily on the industrial heartland of West Germany. Visibility in Essen fell below fifty metres. People at risk from heart attacks, bronchial spasms or asthma were told to stay indoors, and routine operations at city hospitals were postponed in case the facilities were needed by a flood of smog victims.

The alert, which brought about the most far-reaching emergency measures to counter smog ever taken in Germany, came at the height of the nation's concern about acid rain. The fear was of a catastrophe such as that in London in 1952. If trees can die, the word went, so can humans.

In the event, there was no great influx to either hospitals or mortuaries along the Ruhr. But the alert galvanized the Germans into establishing the most sophisticated national smog-monitoring and alarm system in the world. It came into force in November 1985. During the first winter there were minor smog alerts in both the Ruhr and Bavaria.

In January 1985 levels of sulphur dioxide reached 1,500 micrograms per cubic metre in the Ruhr. The first national alert is sounded now at 600 micrograms. The chief air-pollution inspector in Nuremberg, Herr Schafaueser, told me that even this is too high. 'The limit was set by a federal commission on which the representatives from northern states said there should not be too many alerts,' he said.

Sulphur dioxide in the air and smog deaths

4,500 micrograms/m³	Peak of London smog, 1952: 4,000 dead
3,000 micrograms/m³	Peak of London smog, 1962: 700 dead
1,500 micrograms/m³	Peak of Ruhr smog, January 1985
1,000 micrograms/m³	Short-term peaks in London, February 1985
600 micrograms/m³	First German warnings sounded Caused small increases in death rates in London in 1950s
400 micrograms/m³	Bronchial attacks increase
300 micrograms/m³	First Nuremberg alert

So Nuremberg puts out its first warning when sulphur dioxide hits 300 micrograms in a cubic metre of air. The Nuremberg system came into effect on 19 February 1986. Within a week, there had been two alerts in which people were asked to leave their cars at home and turn down their thermostats. Few did, says Schafaueser.

Such a 'mini-smog' would have seemed tame indeed to Londoners a generation ago. But German doctors say that people with heart or lung disease are at risk whenever sulphur dioxide rises above 400 micrograms. They can draw on much interesting work from Britain to underline their point.

For damage to lungs, as for damage to buildings, Britain is the greatest open-air laboratory in the world. A series of studies conducted in Britain in the 1960s by the Medical Research Council are still central to arguments about what is safe and what is not. Most of the findings underline the point that you do not need a 1952-style smog before people start dying.

Lesser smogs in London since 1952 raised both death rates and hospital admissions. In December 1962, ten years almost to the day after the great smog, levels of sulphur dioxide reached 3,000 micrograms per cubic metre in London. That was only two-thirds of the 1952 peak (though twice that of the Ruhr smog of 1985). The death rate in London during the smog of 1962 doubled for the duration. There were at least 700 extra deaths.[27]

Later the same winter, in the last week of January, the death rate in London jumped by 60 per cent during another smog when sulphur dioxide levels reached 1,200 micrograms.[28] Similarly, in the winter of 1958-9, scientists from the Medical Research Council found a link between periods of high pollution and death rates and hospital admissions. Concentrations of sulphur dioxide exceeded 600 micrograms (the new German alert level) on ten days that winter. The days were all among the thirteen with the highest death tolls in the capital.

Since the early 1960s, smogs have been rare in London and day-by-day links between pollution and death rates are now much less marked. But when scientists look at the statistics on illnesses they see a picture that remains alarming. A study of 1,000 men in north London found that the number of them suffering bronchial attacks rose whenever smoke and sulphur dioxide levels both rose above 400 micrograms.

During three winters in the 1960s, the Medical Research Council asked 2,000 bronchitic patients in London to keep diaries of how they felt each day. They were told to record whether they felt better, worse or the same as the previous day. The researchers found what they describe as a 'remarkable correlation' with concentrations of both smoke and sulphur dioxide. In the winter of 1959–60, the five worst days for the bronchitics proved to be the five days when sulphur dioxide rose above 600 micrograms. In 1964–5, the four worst days for the bronchitics were all among the handful of days when sulphur dioxide rose above 500 micrograms. In the final winter of the study, 1969–70, there was one day when sulphur dioxide exceeded 600 micrograms. It produced the second high illness 'score' among the bronchitics.

With the decline of the great smogs the massacres seem to be over. The Medical Research Council's air-pollution unit has been shut down, but the council keeps churning out figures that suggest the steady loss of life goes on. The death rate for bronchitis remains at least twice as high in British cities as in the countryside.[29] The contrast – an extreme version of a phenomenon seen all over the world – does not go away when statisticians adjust their calculations to allow for smoking, the biggest single cause of bronchitis. And the difference is the same for women as for men, which shows that factory work is not a big factor.

A standard measure of the health of a person's lungs is the amount of air they can expel in a single breath. It is a good indicator of encroaching lung disease. In the mid-1960s British scientists used the test to compare the lungs of post-men in central London with those in the country towns of Gloucester, Peterborough and Norwich.[30] They found that the lungs of London's postmen were 10 per cent less efficient. Another study found that the incidence of death from bronchitis among bus drivers was greater in the most polluted boroughs of London than in cleaner ones.

There is growing evidence that children are especially at risk. Doctors in Duisburg, an ugly steel town in the Ruhr, say that when pollution intensifies, children under four years old suffer more from infectious laryngitis and bronchitis. In a big study of children in Sheffield in the 1960s, five-year-olds were twice as likely to have persistent coughs and other lung problems if they lived in the most polluted suburb, Attercliffe, than if they lived in the cleanest, Greenhill.[31] Differences in class between residents in the two areas did not influence the finding. Follow-ups of British children adopted at birth show three times as many infections of the lung among children who live in cities as among their country brothers and sisters.[32]

In recent years, the physiology of how the great London smogs killed has become clearer. Doctors believe that exceptionally large droplets of sulphuric acid overwhelmed the power of natural ammonia in the nose and throats of victims to neutralize the acid.[33] It invaded the deeper passages where the final defence, mucus, was produced in such quantities that the victims choked and died. What nobody knows is whether this process is a killer at lower concentrations of acid and with smaller droplets. Some doctors say that the ammonia, produced by bacteria in the throat, is quite sufficient to cope with modern levels of acid pollution. But the US government's Environmental Protection Agency says that acid in the air in a typical US city could be dangerous. People doing manual labour out of doors may breathe far faster and their throats may not be able to neutralize all the acid that they breathe. Wheezing children running in from play may have breathed dangerous quantities of acid deep into their lungs. There is probably only a tenth of a second during which acid air being inhaled can be neutralized. But US scientists say that under some circumstances the job could take five seconds. Bizarrely, bad teeth may help. The bacteria in dental plaques make ammonia, so good teeth might sometimes be bad for lungs.[34]

The year of London's worst smog was also the year Los Angeles discovered a new pollution phenomenon – ozone, generated in bright summer sunlight from the products of car exhausts. Ozone irritates the throat and lungs. It causes catarrh, headaches and a reduced resistance to infections. Some of the symptoms might be mistaken for hay fever and are likely to occur when ozone levels rise above eighty parts per billion for an hour or more (a level found on sunny summer days all over both urban and rural Europe). Canadian scientists say that when ozone levels are high, more children are admitted to hospital with severe asthma attacks.[35] On days when ozone levels exceed eighty parts per billion in air, asthma attacks among children were double the summer average. In late 1986, the Environmental Protection Agency agreed that ozone exacerbated lung disease, and pointed out that hospital admissions rise with ozone levels.

Ozone and sulphur dioxide may act in a deadly tandem. Non-smoking Canadian students found that they could breathe out only two-thirds as much air after being exposed to a mixture of the two gases which, on their own, had virtually no effect on their breathing.[36] The researchers say: 'We can safely assume that the long-term consequences of such repetitive insults may well result in serious lung damage.' Such effects could clearly undo much of the good work accom plished by past clean-air legislation.

At the height of the worst ozone episode on record in Britain, during the long, hot summer of 1976, deaths leapt by twenty per cent in London. Several hundred people died in addition to the expected toll. Everybody assumed the heat was to blame. But was it really ozone? We do not know. That year the Medical Research Council's air-pollution research unit was preparing to be shut down. No serious study of the summer deaths was carried out.

Crumbling Edifices

The Acropolis in Athens is the greatest surviving monument of ancient Greek civilization. Its buildings, including the Parthenon, were built from the best marble on a hilltop above the city around 400 BC. Today, pollution from the burgeoning metropolis of Athens is destroying its greatest asset. Professor Theo Skoulikidis, from the National Technical University of Athens, was called in to assess the damage. He says: 'The severe deterioration begun in the last twenty to twenty-five years coincides with the beginning of the intense industrialization of the Athens area. The pollution caused, during this period, more deterioration than the exposure of the monuments for 2,400 years without it.'[37]

Conservators are taking the monument apart, repairing it and putting it back together again. But some parts are so badly damaged that they may never return to the open air. The original caryatids, giant marble pillars carved in the shape of women, are now in air-conditioned cases in the Acropolis Museum. What tourists see outside are replicas.

Athens is home to half the population of Greece and more than half of its factories and cars. It is western Europe's most polluted city. During the frequent smogs, driving in the city is rationed. There is a permanent ban on fuel oils with a high sulphur content and tourists' buses are kept off the top of the Acropolis hill. But still the destruction escalates.

The polluting gases dissolve in water that collects on the

surface of the marble, turning it acid. The acid burns into the marble, converting it to gypsum. Rain washes off the gypsum and with it all detail from statues and other architectural flourishes. If the stone is sheltered from rain, the gypsum will form a brittle crust which eventually flakes off.

Often, statues that look in reasonable condition are largely composed of undisturbed gypsum. Skoulikidis says that the gypsum on the women of the caryatids must be preserved at all costs, 'otherwise they will be bald because their hair is now all gypsum'.

Venice, another of Europe's jewels, has 'an exceptionally high rate of stone damage', according to Professor Marco Del Monte, Italy's leading specialist on stone decay.[38] He has spent ten years investigating the state of Venice's monuments. Old photographs show that in Venice, as in Athens, 'the stone decay did not actually set in until after the Second World War,' he says. But today it eats away at this unique city at a rate greater even than in Milan. Nobody can explain this. Venice is much less polluted than Milan, a notoriously dirty city. There are no cars on the island centre of the city and the rain is less acid than in most of Italy. Outside Venice, however, there is a large industrial area nearby. Del Monte and his colleagues believe black carbon particles from this zone, where fuel oil with a high sulphur content is burned, could be a potent factor in the decay.

In Venice, and all over Italy, priceless Renaissance frescos are beginning to break up. The Giotto frescos in Padua and the Andrea del Sarto frescos in Florence, both world famous, have been investigated in detail.[39] Frescos are created by painting on wet plaster. Now pustules are forming in the plaster. The pustules are composed of gypsum and few doubt that acid fallout is to blame.

John Larson, the chief conservator at the Victoria and Albert Museum in London, has plenty of experience of the decay of Italian monuments. In the 1960s he helped pioneer conservation in Florence and Venice. Today, back in London, he spends much of his time trying to rescue some of the hundreds of marble statues brought back from Italy over the centuries by travelling English gentlemen.

A typical example on display at the museum came from Rome in 1702 and was put in St James's Gardens in central London. It was 'brought inside' to the Victoria and Albert, cracked and eroded by London air, twenty years ago. 'Once the decay breaks the surface and cracks form, the marble decays right through and loses its strength,' says Larson. 'That is why arms fall off these statues a lot.'

Larson's prize exhibit is *Neptune and Triton*, a statue by Bernini, which spent many decades in the gardens of Castle Howard. The castle is miles from anywhere, on the edge of the Yorkshire wolds. Yet, says Larson, acid attack has taken its toll. 'We found that the porosity of the stone was three times greater on the back, which received rain, as on the front, which did not. There were so many holes that when we tried to paint on a preservative, it flowed right through an arm and oozed out of the other side.' Even so, he says, 'if this sculpture were up for sale it would go for millions.'

Larson has little doubt that it is modern pollution, and especially acid rain, that is to blame. When I visited him in his laboratory in the bowels of the museum, he was examining the sculpture of a knight, first erected 700 years ago. In a few well-sheltered places, the original gilt paint had survived. 'The more we analyse these sculptures, the more we are finding how resistant they were to unpolluted air,' he says. 'Many medieval churches were painted all over. To do that you had to believe it would last. Today, such paint would be decaying within a decade.'

'In India, you can still see perfectly preserved marble,' says Larson. 'This is impossible anywhere in Europe. The marble fronts of the posh Arab banks here have to be re-polished every couple of years.' When Larson put marble samples on the roof of the Victoria and Albert, the polish etched off within four weeks. Another sample, put on the roof twenty years ago, has disintegrated entirely. 'We have very little hope of maintaining any stone sculpture in any external environment without it suffering radical damage that will eventually render it valueless, both historically and aesthetically,' he says.

It used to be assumed that sulphur dioxide was the only

pollutant that damaged marble statues and buildings made of the chemically identical limestone. Britain, where sulphur dioxide levels have fallen so drastically, should be the best place in the world to test this theory. Yet when in 1984 the House of Commons environment committee studied acid rain in Britain, one of its most important findings was that, all over Britain, the decay of marble and limestone showed no sign of decline.[40] Indeed it seemed to be getting worse.

Lincoln Cathedral is in the path of pollution from the battery of power stations in the Trent valley. Its architects say: 'The recent acceleration in the deterioration of the stone-work, particularly that of the Romanesque and medieval statuary, is due to acid rain.' At Chichester Cathedral in Sussex, 'the greater part of the external masonry cladding the central tower and spire is failing due to atmospheric attack.' The surveyor of conservation at the National Trust, which owns more than two hundred important historic buildings and vast amounts of garden sculpture, says 'erosion of stone is on the increase'.

Ian Stewart, an architect responsible for monitoring several historic buildings, says: 'Many of our most valuable stone buildings are suffering from accelerating decay of their most characteristic features. Exquisite and irreplaceable medieval craftsmanship, which has endured for centuries, is literally disintegrating before our eyes.' At Beverley Minster in Yorkshire, 'the decay is indiscriminate and some stones added during eighteenth-, nineteenth- and even twentieth-century repairs are in a worse condition than original thirteenth-century works,' he says.

When William Waldegrave, the environment minister, opened a debate on acid rain in Parliament in 1985, he spoke most eloquently about Wells Cathedral in Somerset – perhaps because his father, Lord Waldegrave, is chairman of the Friends of Wells Cathedral.[41] 'The magnificent west front has rightly been called the greatest collection of medieval sculpture north of the Alps. That stone has been terribly damaged,' he said. He had no doubt that pollution is responsible.

Westminster Abbey in London is one of Europe's most

visited 'medieval' buildings. Yet most of the stone on the outside is not medieval. It has been replaced by modern Portland stone. Recent renovation has cost £5 million. Forty-four flying buttresses, which were rebuilt ninety years ago, now require replacement, and roof pinnacles put up in the 1950s are already being replaced. John Larson calls this 'Disney World architecture'. Nothing is what it seems. Everything is an imitation.

St Paul's Cathedral in the City of London is made of highly resistant Portland stone. Its survival during the Second World War, when most of the buildings around it were flattened in air raids, became a symbol of national resistance. But there is no defence against acid fallout. Robert Porter, the surveyor of the fabric, says today: 'Mouldings that had been replaced within the last century or so are again in need of restoration. The ornate gate piers of the South Portico have deteriorated to such an extent that it is now necessary to remove them for their preservation.'[42] They have been replaced by facsimiles. 'Nothing,' says Porter, 'can prevent the destruction of carvings and other vulnerable detail in exposed positions from acidic attack, short of the elimination of the pollutants.'

The only serious attempts to measure whether decay is as bad today as in the past have been made by students from University College London, on St Paul's Cathedral. David Sharp, who has a good head for heights, scaled the balustrade high up on the cathedral to do his research.[43] When the balustrade was built in 1718, stone was hoisted up on pulleys held by holes drilled into stone. When building was finished, the holes were filled with molten lead. Sharp found that today the lead plugs jut out three centimetres above the eroded stone. In the intervening 250 years, during which London suffered continuous heavy pollution, the top of the balustrade eroded at an average of 0.08 millimetres per year. Sharp then measured the current rate of erosion on St Paul's using an instrument known as a micro-erosion meter. The average erosion over five years from 1980 to 1985 was 0.14 millimetres per year – almost twice the average of the past 250 years. When he estimated erosion from the amount of rock residues in rainwater running off the balustrade, he came up with an even higher figure of 0.22 millimetres.[44]

Lord Marshall has an office in the City with splendid views overlooking St Paul's. Should his organization take some blame for its decay? Gerald Gibbs, Marshall's specialist on buildings, insists not. He blames the 'memory effect' of past pollution. The gypsum formed on the surface of the stone years ago will carry on burrowing into the stone, when pollution at the surface has abated, he says. Gibbs says the memory effect could last fifty years. The effect certainly exists; but how important is it? New stone exposed to today's pollution – at York Minster for instance – has been found to decay almost as fast as old stone.

An important clue to what is going on comes from a study by scientists at the government's Building Research Establishment. They left samples of stone in different places around south-east England for two years. The stone sheltered from rain eroded at only half the rate of stone exposed to rain.[45] The differing amounts of sulphur dioxide in rural and urban air did not seem to have much influence at all. It begins to look as if acid from electricity power stations could indeed be important.

It used to be assumed that acid rain was not acid enough to damage stone and that sulphur dioxide dissolving on stone surfaces was more corrosive. But laboratory tests show that limestone dissolves seventy-five times faster in typical modern rain (pH 4) than in unpolluted rain (pH 5.25).[46] This suggests both the importance of acid rain and the likelihood that a few highly acid storms might do most of the damage. Cue for the indomitable Alan Sharp, who clambered out on to St Paul's during a couple of thunderstorms. He found extremely acid rain and 'very, very high rates of erosion of stone'.

Acid rain now stands accused of accelerating the decay of Britain's most-loved buildings. But it should not be in the dock alone. Are the nitrogen oxides from cars blameless? Gibbs at the generating board blusters about coaches parked outside St Paul's Cathedral all day in summer with their engines on. This may be trite, but Roy Butlin at the Building

Research Establishment believes nitrogen oxides from vehicles 'might play a role. But the mechanism is still very open.'

Some scientists in Italy and the USA say that the distinctive, tiny particles of fly ash blown out of the chimneys of power stations may have an important effect, catalyzing the conversion of sulphur dioxide to sulphuric acid on the surface of stone.[47] But extraordinarily little is known about these processes or their importance. The standard British textbook in this field was written in the 1930s – long before either car exhausts or acid rain were issues.[48] As the MPs wrote in their report: 'It seems to have been presumed that when the Clean Air Act removed most visible pollution, the need for research on the effects of air pollution on buildings ended . . . this shortcoming is to be deplored.'[40]

The MPs' stricture applies with even more force to bricks and mortar than to limestone buildings. Bricks are porous and can be attacked in much the same way as limestone. In cities, many older buildings have heavily pitted bricks. Repointing of mortar is a familiar activity for city-dwellers. Does pollution speed the decay? Nobody knows because nobody has troubled to find out.

The signs are not good. Tower blocks are scrutinized more closely than most buildings because of the fear that they might fall down. When, during 1985, Birmingham city council examined a series of six large blocks in Erdington, the city engineer found 'unacceptable levels of sulphates' in the mortar joints of the brickwork. Air pollution was the only likely cause. He ordered that all the brickwork on the blocks should be replaced. Is similar decay happening elsewhere? Nobody knows.

A meeting of the American Chemical Society in 1985 dipped its toe in the water. It heard that 'acid rain affects brick masonry by selectively dissolving the glassy fabric that holds the silica grains of a brick together. The resulting salts migrate through the porous brick. Salts are deposited wherever the water evaporates, leaving a white powdery film that appears to ooze out of the masonry. Eventually all that is left is a weakened silica sponge.'[49]

*

The 'blue miracle' of Chartres Cathedral in northern France is gone – a victim, it seems, of acid rain. Gottfried Frenzel, who runs the Institute for Stained Glass Research in West Germany, says thousands of other medieval stained-glass windows, from York to Venice, could be ruined within a generation.[50]

Chartres Cathedral contains more than 2,000 square metres of stained glass, all dating from the twelfth and thirteenth century, when the art reached its height in France. 'As recently as twenty years ago,' says Frenzel, 'one could marvel at the glass, and in particular at the richness achieved in the predominantly blue panes of the Romanesque and Gothic periods.' Today, he says, 'the contrast is shocking.' The intensity of the blue is fading and 'the panes of other colours have corroded and turned a mangy brown, rendering the stained-glass images barely recognizable.'

In Canterbury Cathedral there are etched pits in stained glass in the great west window and the Trinity and Corona chapels. 'The pits have perforated the panels, leaving them quite porous, so that acid rain can reach the inner surface of the glass and eat into the paintwork there,' says Frenzel. The glass at Cologne Cathedral 'looks like sheets of chalky plaster' from the outside, he says.

Continuous etching by air pollutants has corroded the exterior surface of the glass, reducing its thickness year by year and giving the decomposed surface a weathering crust. The process of destruction starts anew as each rain washes the crust away. Meanwhile, the coloured glass breaks into tiny particles. The particles fall out of each panel; thus the window disintegrates.

The martyrs' window in Augsburg Cathedral in West Germany was installed in 1130. In 1943, photographs show it in perfect condition. But today it is pitted and discoloured.[46]

In 1984, a study for the United Nations' Economic Commission for Europe concluded that acid rain was having a 'disastrous effect' on the continent's stained glass. Since the 1950s, deterioration of medieval glass 'has apparently accelerated to the extent that a total loss is expected within a few decades, if no remedial action is taken.' More modern glass is less at risk because it is more homogeneous and has a fire-polished surface which resists corrosion.

The scientific debate about what is damaging medieval glass is poor. Little serious research has been done, and the main participants have not grasped the nature of the polluted environment whose effects they are trying to assess. Most of the argument has centred on the effect of sulphur dioxide gas. A school of German scientists say that the gas attacks the glass, etching holes and combining with chemical components of the glass. They say that a gypsum crust then forms, which completes the physical destruction of the glass. Britain's top expert, Professor Roy Newton, says this is rubbish. There is always gypsum in the surface of glass, he says. But there is no evidence that it penetrates deep into the glass, where the destruction begins. The real destructive agent, he says, is water, which will attack the glass without the help of pollution.[51] It seeks out chemicals such as potassium, sodium and calcium in the glass and, chemically, 'sucks' them to the surface.

Newton says the glass from Canterbury, York and elsewhere is decaying now because it was stored badly during the Second World War. Canterbury's glass was kept in a sealed crypt where it was probably permanently wet for four years. At York, he says, the glass stored wet is now in a worse state than the glass stored dry.

Newton's case seems strong. If sulphur dioxide pollution were the real culprit, why were the effects so late in appearing in Britain? London has had severe sulphur pollution since the seventeenth century. But both sides have failed to ask if acid rain itself has a role. It has been left to Dr J. F. Feenstra from the Free University Amsterdam to point out that acid water greatly speeds up the movement of potassium and the other chemicals through the glass to the surface.[46] The more acid the rain, the faster the migration and the faster the destruction of the glass. That, perhaps, is why it is the post-war years, in which sulphur dioxide pollution has dwindled in towns but rain has become more acid everywhere, that have seen the destruction of medieval glass. If so, nowhere in

Europe is safe. And the medieval glass may, as Frenzel predicts, disappear within a generation.

The army had to be called in when the main water pipe supplying Leeds burst. For four days just before Christmas 1985, a quarter of a million people in the Yorkshire city were without water. So were twenty schools and two hospitals. The metre-wide pipe was heavily corroded and sprang a leak which turned into a flood, releasing almost three million litres of water before Yorkshire Water could stem the flow. Two standby pipes stood by unused because their valves were so corroded they could not be turned on.

Nobody mentioned acid rain at the time. But without it, corrosion would have been much less severe, and Yorkshire Water would not be facing an eventual bill for replacing corroded water mains (preferably before they burst) that could approach half a billion pounds.

There are more than a quarter of a million kilometres of water mains in England. The great majority are made of iron, which acid water corrodes. According to the water authorities, half of the water put into the mains is acid and half the mains network is corroding away. Yet, the industry's engineers at the Water Research Centre say that 'acid rain and its bearing on water mains corrosion is not a specific aspect of our current research programme. This is because acid rain is not currently perceived to be a problem in this context.'[52] They are convinced, despite considerable evidence to the contrary, that all the acid in Britain's water mains is natural.

Tens of thousands of kilometres of Britain's leaky water mains badly need repairs if they are not to suffer the fate of the Leeds pipe. The Water Research Centre admits that a crisis could arise in which 'in default of remedial action, half of the entire length of iron mains would fail in a period of twenty years.'[53]

North West Water, which supplies the west side of the Pennines, says 40 per cent of its mains already 'suffer from an unacceptable degree of corrosion'. Lancashire tap-water is often dirty and loaded with bits of rusty iron. Yorkshire towns ouch as Sheffield, Leeds and Huddersfield suffer the the same. Corrosion is worst in towns supplied with water from the most acid reservoirs. Today Yorkshire Water says that around Halifax (where acid fallout meant trees would not grow for the Forestry Commission) every unlined iron water main needs renovating.[54]

Further south, Severn Trent Water says that in more than 4,000 kilometres of its iron mains, corrosion blisters take up more than half the theoretical capacity of the pipes.[55] The towns worst hit are Birmingham, which is supplied from the headwaters of the river Severn in Wales, and Derby, which is supplied from the southern Pennines.

Back above ground, many other vital pieces of the nation's metal infrastructures are corroded by acid fallout. Zinc galvanizing is coated on to iron to protect it from rust – but acid fallout will corrode the zinc. In 1964, the Central Electricity Generating Board strung galvanized metal cans from transmission towers along the national grid. It wanted to look for the corrosive effects of emissions from its power stations.[56] The resulting map showed high rates of corrosion downwind of several of the board's power stations. The map was never published, and when one of the board's engineers, Tom Shaw, proposed setting up a permanent network of cans his superiors turned him down. Shaw eventually did the work himself, finding funds from British Rail (which is interested in potential corrosion of transmission wires as it electrifies its line from King's Cross to Edinburgh), the Ministry of Agriculture (which pays subsidies to farmers for replacing galvanized fences damaged by corrosion) and the Construction Industry Research and Information Association (which would rather its members' bridges and towers did not fall down).

Shaw found that the zinc on his cans corrodes in proportion to the local concentrations of sulphur in the air. In recent years, the rate of corrosion has not fallen in line with sulphur dioxide levels, however. The likely explanation is that today the wet deposition of sulphur in acid rain is an important factor in corrosion of metals in the air.

For most metals, wetness is a key element in the rate of

corrosion. Only wet metal absorbs the atmospheric pollutants. Iron, for instance, barely rusts at all unless the humidity gets above 80 per cent. Then, pure air still fails to induce rusting, but wet air polluted with sulphur dioxide sends rust rates soaring. A study in the 1960s found rusting of steel plate in the 'steel town' of Sheffield to be five times higher than in Llanwrtyd Wells in Wales, and ten times higher than in northern Sweden.[57] A committee set up by the British government at that time concluded that corrosion cost at least 3.5 per cent of the gross national product.[58] The exercise has not been repeated.

The church bells of Holland do not sound as pure as they once did. The evidence comes from the Utrecht Dom tower. The peal, or carillon, there is one of twenty in Holland cast by François and Pieter Hemony in the seventeenth century. They were famous for their perfect tuning and sonority, and nobody else's work has attained their quality since. But in recent years 'false notes and lesser richness in sound of the Hemony carillons' caused concern, according to Professor Feenstra of Amsterdam.[46] Detailed analysis of the sound quality has found that, since 1951, when the carillon was 'practically undamaged', there has been a serious decline, especially among the smaller bells. Corrosion is being blamed.

Most bells are made of a version of bronze that is about 80 per cent copper. When copper is corroded it forms a hard coating, known as a patina, which is often green. The patina normally stops further corrosion. But bells are constantly being vibrated (it is that which produces the sound), and this vibration shakes the hard patina loose; bits fall off and further corrosion will occur behind the patina. For small, high-quality bells, this is serious. For 300 years the Utrecht carillon retained its perfection. In thirty years, it has deteriorated.

Bronze used to be regarded as safe from pollution. But it is now clear that bronze cannot cope with modern forms of atmospheric attack. In Venice, the four bronze horses of San Marco were first erected outside the Basilica of San Marco 700 years ago. After that they moved around a lot. Napoleon once took them to Paris. But at the end of the Second World War they were back, looking as good as new, high up on the façade of the basilica. Since then, they have been attacked by something new in the Venice air. Attempts to restore them began in 1974, but today the horses have been taken indoors for protection. What visitors see in St Mark's Square are replicas.

In Britain, copper is being eaten away on church roofs all over the country. From Liverpool Cathedral to St Augustine's, Bexhill in Sussex, acid rain is being blamed for perished copper roofs.[59] The copper hooks that held the slates to roofs all over Europe until a few years ago are deteriorating as acid fallout destroys their patina.

The British Library houses more than ten million books – virtually every title published in Britain. This priceless collection is being eaten away by pollution because most of the books are kept in London. David Clements, the director of the library's preservation service, says that books last roughly half as long in London as they would in the countryside, away from gaseous pollutants. At the new British Library, now being built at St Pancras, £30 million is to be spent creating such an environment by artificial means.

Paper absorbs both sulphur dioxide and nitrogen dioxide. The gases make the paper acid. As more pollution is absorbed the paper becomes brown and brittle. First, dog-eared corners fall off, then the paper begins to crumble. In the 1960s, F. L. Hudson looked at identical books preserved for more than two centuries at two libraries: the Portico library in the heart of Manchester and at Chatsworth House in the Derbyshire Peak District. The oldest book held in both libraries was *Historiae Normannorum Scriptores Antiqui* by A. Duchesne, published in 1619. In the Chatsworth copy the exposed top edge of the paper had a pH of 4.4. In Portico it had a pH of 3.2, making it more than ten times more acid. Of twenty-six pairs of books examined, virtually all showed a similar variation.[46]

Acid slowly destroys the strings of cellulose molecules that make up paper. Old paper, made from rags, lasts best. Paper from the past hundred years is worst. It is made from wood pulp and may contain its own acid. So, while the British Library's Gutenberg Bible is still in good condition after years of exposure to London air, pulp paperbacks from the 1960s already look bad. When Clements took a copy of *Guns at Sulphur Creek*, by H. C. Averill, from the vaults, its paper was well browned and when he bent back the corner of a page, it broke. Five per cent of the books in the library's collection break in this way, says Clements – that is more than half a million books.

Leather bindings also decay under acid attack. From 1950 to 1970, two sets of 200 different leather bindings were stored and monitored; one set in the British Library in London, the other at the National Library of Wales in Aberystwyth. Decay was much worse in London.[46] Some materials used in tanning leather react with air pollution to form acids that eat away the leather, causing cracking and crumbling. The disease is known as 'red rot'. Sulphuric acid constituted up to 8 per cent of the decaying leather in books sampled at the British Library in the 1930s.

Many other 'indoor' materials react like paper or leather to sulphur dioxide. Cotton and linen are derived from plants and made largely of cellulose. They respond like paper. Silk, wool and parchment are made of animal proteins and rot like leather. Synthetic materials may succumb too. The women of Britain who spent the 1950s and 1960s complaining that their nylon stockings 'ran' within days of purchase never knew that air pollution was the cause.

As sulphur dioxide has declined in importance, so nitrogen dioxide with its similarly acidifying effect has increased. Now, ozone is becoming a menace, too. Ozone is an oxidant. It reacts with all organic materials – paper, leather, paintings, textiles, furniture, biological specimens, fur – with great speed. This, says Garry Thomson, the chief conservator at the National Gallery in London until 1985, makes ozone 'extremely dangerous in the museum'.

For some time, scientists were seduced by the knowledge that levels of ozone inside museums and other buildings were much lower than outside. In the summer of 1973 Thomson recorded ozone levels outside the National Gallery in

Trafalgar Square of 100 parts per billion. Inside, they were less than one part per billion. Then as Thomson records in his classic book, *The Museum Environment*, someone asked why.[39] The answer was that the exhibits were absorbing the ozone. One study of a bedroom found that curtains, bedclothes and the like ensured that ozone had a 'half life' with the windows shut of just six minutes.

Ozone destroys the material, often by making it brittle, so that it cracks and crumbles. Thus fabrics lose their strength and tear, and paints with organic binders erode. Manufacturers of car tyres have spent hundreds of millions of pounds on rubbers that do not crack under the impact of ozone. The manufacturers of rubber bands have not. That is why they snap so often and so unexpectedly. Ozone also causes many dyes in textiles to fade and pigments in artists' paint may suffer similarly. As ozone levels in Europe continue to rise, Thomson has one solace for museums. People absorb and destroy ozone every time they breathe in. So the more visitors there are in museums, the less ozone will be left in the air to destroy the exhibits.

3 Acid Waters

Rain, Rivers and Soils

Gjermund Seldal was born at the beginning of the century – before the fish in Norway began to die. He lived at Dolemo on the river Tovdal, which had always been the least acid of the seven rivers that drain southern Norway. In 1926, as neighbouring rivers were losing fish, the local inspector of fisheries called the waters there naturally neutral. 'This river has not had the great reduction in salmon fisheries that is found in most rivers in the southern counties.'[1] Fifty years later, in 1975, the Tovdal was no longer neutral. The salmon, which are extremely sensitive to acid waters, could no longer survive. But the brown trout still swam in great numbers beneath the bridge close to Seldal's home.

On 23 March 1975, as the ice that covered the Tovdal began to melt, Seldal saw three dead fish from the bridge. Day by day, as the ice cleared, he saw more dead trout floating in the river. Alarmed, he called in scientists from the University of Oslo. Ivar Muniz was one of the first on the scene.

We arrived on 4 April and quickly found between sixty and eighty dead trout within 150 metres of the bridge. We caught three more, lethargic but still alive, in small nets. They were so poorly, we could pick them out of the water. When we put them in tanks, they tipped over on their sides. They had lost all equilibrium.

Muniz brought in frogmen. Upstream at a pool called Toftefjorden they found 5,000 dead trout. Gulls were sitting on the ice, waiting to pick dead fish from the water. 'It was a massacre,' says Muniz. 'Something had completely eradicated a huge proportion of the fish along almost thirty kilometres of the Tovdal. We reckon there was one dead trout for every five square metres of river.'

Vets could find no damage to the organs of the fish, or any obvious cause of death. But when Muniz examined the living specimens back in the lab, he found that they had very little sodium in their blood. This is a typical symptom of acid poisoning. The acid had poisoned the gills of the fish, making them unable to extract salt from the water to maintain the sodium levels in their bodies.

Spring is a dangerous season for Norway's surviving fish. The snows on the mountains melt swiftly, rushing into swollen rivers. With the snow comes four or five months of accumulated pollution. The rivers become very acid. As he began his investigations into the spectacular fish kill on the Tovdal, Muniz discovered that the pH of the stretches of river with the most dead trout had dropped from 5.2 to 4.6. Some tributary streams recorded a pH as low as 4.0. In such conditions, says Muniz, 'it takes only two or three days to kill a fish. There is no doubt that the Tovdal massacre was a prime example of the lethal effects of acid rain.' In the four years following the Tovdal massacre, the number of brown trout in the whole length of the river dropped to a tenth of its former total. Muniz says that the decline continues today.

Until recently, the loss of river fish in Norway had been confined to the far south of the country. Today western Norway is suffering too. During four successive spring snowmelts, from 1981 to 1984, scientists found dead salmon and trout in the River Vikedal near Bergen.[2] The acid, they say, is spreading down from the vulnerable upland streams to lower lakes and rivers. The fish are also starting to die further downstream than before. It seems that over the years the rivers are losing their ability to neutralize acid. Alkaline elements such as calcium, which are washed out from the soils, are being used up. This seems to be happening even though the amount of acid fallout from the skies may be starting to fall.

Muniz helped to conduct a series of detailed studies of coastal lakes around Lake Selura in southern Norway from 1976 to 1983. Landowners in the nearby uplands had started to notice the disappearance of fish in the 1950s. But at that time, fish survived in all the lowland lakes. Now, in some of those lakes, they are on the verge of extinction.[3] In Lake Djupvikvatn, the researchers could find only two arctic char in 1982. They were nine and fourteen years old.

One disturbing feature of the death of lakes all over the world is that, as the waters become more acid, anglers are amazed at the large size of the fish they catch. This has happened at Lake Selura. In 1976, the arctic char here were stunted and often appeared sick. Since then they have become bigger and healthier. In 1976, none were longer than twenty-one centimetres; by 1982, more than half were longer than this. This will not last. Acid waters are killing the young fry in the lake and the proportion of the fish over ten years old increased during the study from 4 per cent to 40 per cent. These older fish are basking in the luxury of having few younger competitors to take their food. When they die, the fishery may be gone for ever.

In the late 1970s, the Norwegian scientists began to suspect that acid was not the only thing killing the fish. The critical pH below which fish could not survive in a stream varied by a unit or more. The missing factor turned out to be aluminium – in particular some forms of soluble, inorganic aluminium. Acid waters dissolve the aluminium from soils and wash it into streams, where it kills fish.

Aluminium kills by upsetting the operation of a fish's gills, causing them to clog with mucus. The disruption reduces the amount of oxygen that gets into the fish's blood. Aluminium seems to be most poisonous when there is little calcium in the water. Scientists now see acid, aluminium and shortages of calcium as the three determining factors in the extinction of fish.[4] In the upland streams and lakes of southern Norway, all three factors come together.

Acid lakes can be very beautiful. They are usually crystal clear. Luscious carpets of green algae cover the boulders at their edge. Lake bottoms may be overgrown with moss. All this green is deceptive. In a normal lake the greenery would be decomposing in a cycle that provides nutrients for other living things in the water. In acid lakes decomposition is very slow. The whole metabolism of the lake is slowed down.

Scientists from the Canadian department of fisheries spent eight years, from 1975, dumping sulphuric acid into a small lake in Ontario to find out what happened as the pH sunk year by year.[5] The lake is known simply as Lake 223 to preserve its anonymity and prevent anyone with a tanker-load of toilet cleaner from messing up the experiment. The pH of the lake has fallen from 6.8 (almost neutral) to around 5. Among the first organisms to disappear were shrimps and minnows. Within a year, at a pH of 5.9, the population of opossum shrimp in the lake fell from seven million almost to nothing. The fathead minnow failed to reproduce and died out a year later.

Meanwhile, new, young trout were failing to appear. At a pH of 5.8, important organisms in the trout's food chain were wiped out. This, the researchers wrote later, was a clear sign 'that irreversible stresses on aquatic ecosystems occur earlier in the acidification process than was heretofore believed'. At pH 5.1, the scientists noticed cannibalism among the trout 'probably because of the scarcity of minnows ... that are normal prey for large trout'. Snails were gone, so too were leeches and mayfly, which had once been abundant.

At a pH of 5.6, the external skeletons of crayfish softened and the fish soon became infested with a parasite. Their eggs were overrun by fungi. The following year, with the pH down to 5.1, the crayfish had virtually disappeared.

Some species flourished. Mayflies were replaced by epidemics of all manner of midges. But by the end of the experiment, none of the major species found in the lake – trout, white suckers, minnows, pearl dace and sculpin – were surviving for more than a few months after hatching.

Since 1983, the scientists have tried to bring the lake back to life. To simulate the effect of a massive cleanup among polluters, they cut by half the amount of acid they dumped. As the acidity of the lake reduced, the suckers and minnows began to reproduce again and the trout grew fatter. It is, they say, 'a habitat brought back from the edge of extinction'.

Ivan Rosenqvist is a tall craggy-faced man. He is seventy years old now and his hands shake. But his conviction is steady. He believes his science has been a victim of politically inspired assassination. The Norwegian government was anxious that I should meet him while I was in Oslo. But only for form's sake. They believe he is a beaten man. Rosenqvist was one of the pioneers of acid-rain science. He spent the early 1970s arguing that foreign pollution was responsible for the death of Norway's fish. But around 1975, he changed his mind. He now says that acid rain has little or nothing to do either with rivers and lakes becoming acid or with the death of fish. 'Reactions in the ground are much more important. Acid rain is a minor factor,' he says.[6]

In the small but highly political world of Norwegian research, such talk smacks of treachery. But Rosenqvist is angry. When government ministers launched a massive research project into acid rain in the early 1970s, they said that the aim was 'to establish the foundations for further negotiations to limit sulphur dioxide emissions in Europe'. Rosenqvist still quotes the phrase to people who visit him in his room at the University of Oslo. 'It was politics, not science,' he says. 'The aim of the research was to find premises for the conclusion. They are trying to reach truth by constant repetition. It seems almost impossible to argue against this dogma now that it has entered the literature.'

Rosenqvist's case is that there is often much more acid naturally present in soils than ever falls out of the skies. Ten times more is typical in southern Norway, he says. And the influence of small changes in methods of agriculture or forestry on the acidity of lakes and streams is 'totally overwhelming even over large changes in the . . . pH of the precipitation water', he says. The source of the extra acid in the waters of southern Norway in recent decades is a build-up of humus in the soil, producing humic acid. The humus developed after farms were deserted in the late nineteenth century (often because people upped sticks and left for the New World), and heather colonized the land.

Rosenqvist has had a sobering effect on some of the more hot-headed scientists-cum-propagandists in Norway. Some of them, says Professor Art Eliassen, a meteorologist specializing in acid-rain research, 'wanted to ignore soil. When

Rosenqvist reminded them of its existence, they got rather angry.' Rosenqvist at his most acerbic puts it this way: 'If you ate a slice of lemon once a month you would certainly be consuming something that was acid. But it is not clear that it would make your urine more acid.'

Rosenqvist asks interesting questions. 'Why is it that during heavy rain, the swollen rivers can be up to fifteen times more acid than the rain? It cannot be the rain alone that is doing it, can it?' While being shunned in Norway, his questions found a ready audience outside, especially in Britain, where the Central Electricity Generating Board had been fighting a long rearguard campaign to under-mine Norwegian demands that it cut sulphur emissions. In 1985, when the board sent a film crew to Norway to pro-duce an educational film the crew spent a day and a half with Rosenqvist, and his is the only Norwegian voice to be heard in the film.[7]

They do not admit it, but to answer Rosenqvist's questions his opponents had to go back to the drawing board. Hans Seip at the University of Oslo admits today: 'The weakest link in the chain from emissions to effects on fish, is still the relationship between deposition and water acidity.' Ivar Muniz says, 'the strongest evidence remains the geographical distribution. The fish have died where the rain is most acid.' But, given Rosenqvist's disturbing questions, they were forced to consider afresh the mechanisms.

Sulphuric acid is composed of two parts, known to chem-ists as ions. The hydrogen ion is the acid bit. The sulphate ion, the other half, is formed from sulphur dioxide by chem-ical transformations in the atmosphere. Seip and his col-leagues returned from the drawing board with the idea that, while the hydrogen ion (the acid) may be important, the sulphate could be even more important. Seip says that it matters very little to streams how much acid builds up in soils unless there is some chemical to take the acid out of the soil and into the water. Even during a snowmelt, runoff waters usually pass briefly through the soil. Sulphate, which was rarely found in soils before the Industrial Revolution, appears to be uniquely good at the job. So natural acid in the soil does not reach rivers in significant amounts until there was sulphate around, too. And that requires acid rain. This argument is now accepted by the Norwegians' arch critics, the scientists at the Central Electricity Generating Board. One of its brightest scientists, Richard Skeffington, says that 'the transfer of acidity into surface waters is dependent on acid deposition because of the role of sulphate'.[8]

There is also growing evidence that both acid and sulphate have been accumulating in Scandinavian soil for many decades. A Swedish study recently repeated an investigation of the acidity of soils carried out in mature forests in the 1920s. The Swedish researchers found that soils today are more than ten times as acid as they were sixty years ago. The work has greatly impressed the CEGB's notoriously sceptical scientists and they cite it as an important reason for their assertion, first made in late 1986, that they now believe acid rain damages Scandinavian soils and surface waters. The acidifcation of Swedish soils is, said the board's top environmental scientist, Peter Chester, 'most reasonably attributable to acid deposition'.

Rosenqvist is adamant that acid rain is not the key. But now his last allies appear to have deserted him. It is the fate of all scientists, however good, to be proved wrong eventually. But, as one of Norway's young campaigning scientists put it: 'It is not easy to be a seventy-year-old scientist and to be proved wrong.'

Norway's case against acid rain has been assembled painstakingly from fragments of evidence. First the fish kills, then the aluminium factor, finally the role of sulphate. Such work may convince scientists but it often leaves politicians and the public confused. Dick Wright, one of the shrewdest of propagandists in Norway's scientific community, knows this. He is an American who has been in Norway for twelve years, working for the Norwegian Institute for Water Research and worrying away at the political dimensions of acid rain. He was the first to suggest that the Norwegians should look for evidence of damage from acid rain in Britain. He went to Galloway in south-west Scotland in 1978, and began a line of study which, as we shall see later, did much to convince British scientists that acid rain could not be ignored.

Now Wright has developed a taste for big experiments, physically big – ones that you can take politicians to see. He has staked out some land, 300 metres up at Risdalsheia, in the mountains of the far south of Norway, where acid fallout is greatest and fish are extinct. He has covered 1,800 square metres of it with a clear acrylic roof and collects the rain so that it can be purified to a 'preindustrial' condition. Inside, the clean rain is sprayed on to the untouched land – 'complete with trees, birds and rabbits,' as Wright puts it. He wants to take this small piece of Norway back to pre-acid days and see what happens. The giant glasshouse sits right at the head of a stream, covering all the land that supplies the stream at its source. Will the water running from the soil into the stream lose its acidity, as Wright expects – or stay the same, as Rosenqvist's ideas suggest?

The Norwegians have invested a lot in this project. The roofs alone cost £200,000. The investment in scientific credibility is high, too. In the first year of operation a thousand visitors were enticed there. Pride of place in Wright's photo album goes to a picture of him showing round Britain's environment minister, William Waldegrave, and his chief scientist, Martin Holdgate. In mid-1986, Lord Marshall paid a visit.

'The project looks like proof to the politicians,' Wright says. Early results did not provide much proof, however. Acidity dropped a little, but sulphate levels remained high. The soils are still 'bleeding old sulphate', he says. 'But we have to know how long that takes.' When the old sulphate from air pollution is gone, he believes, the acidity of the stream will fall. The CEGB believes him and says Wright's work at Risdalsheia is an important reason for its conversion in 1986. But if he is wrong, the Norwegians will have a lot of thinking and explaining to do. And Rosenqvist, in his seventies or not, will be back in business.

The chances of such an upset seem remote. Wright has a second big experiment that is showing quicker results. He has found a piece of 'clean' upland, at Sogndal in the north-west of Norway, where the rain is not yet acid. The site is above the tree-line at 900 metres, a desolate spot with thin, poor soils and a covering of heather. Wright wants to bring this clean site forward in time, to the acid environment experienced today by the southern half of Norway. He sprays the land with sulphuric acid, so mimicking the arrival of acid rain. This produced 'immediate and drastic changes in water chemistry' downstream, says Wright. The pH during snowmelt is down to 4.1 and there are extremely high levels of sulphate and aluminium in the runoff. For Wright, this is 'a direct demonstration that changes to land use are an irrelevance'. Acid raid on its own, without the help of trees or abandoned farms or any other intervention by man or nature, does the damage. He told me in early 1986 that he hoped this was the end of the argument. The CEGB's positive response to his two experiments suggests that it is.

From Galloway to Lochnagar

The Cally Estate was a small paradise for anglers. High in the Galloway hills of south-west Scotland, it attracted a small but regular group of fishermen. Jack Henderson enjoyed his fishing best in Loch Fleet, a small loch on the estate, about 500 metres across. It was a 'connoisseurs' loch', he says, with fewer than ten regular fishermen. Henderson remembers that the fish there were usually larger than in the nearby Loch Grannoch. One glorious week's fishing in the 1940s began with more than forty fish caught from one rod on a Monday. The trick was repeated on the Thursday.[9]

Annual catches in the 1950s were between 100 and 150 trout. But then the fish began to disappear. At the time, they blamed the decline on poaching by miners from the Ayrshire coalfield forty kilometres away. Three times between 1956 and 1964 Murray Usher, who runs the estate, restocked the loch with trout. But the restocking failed and since 1960 only a handful of fish have been caught there. With the fish gone, the estate was sold to the Forestry Commission which has now covered much of the land with conifers.

All over Galloway, similar stories are told. A few trout

remain in nearby Loch Grannoch. But Peter Maitland from the Institute of Terrestrial Ecology, who has investigated this loch, says the fish are getting old and 'in ten years' time, I am willing to bet there will be no fish in Grannoch.'

Four kilometres east is Loch Skerrow. It is now fishless. North-west across the Galloway hills, Loch Enoch lost its fish in the 1930s. In many other lochs in Galloway, fish are vanishing. One macabre sign of decline, first noticed a century ago, is the appearance of tailless trout. Once they appear, says Maitland, the loch is doomed.

The fish are dying because the lakes and streams here have turned acid. Scotland's Freshwater Fisheries Laboratory has charted the change.[10] The pH of Loch Fleet has decreased from 6.6 in 1961 to 4.5. That is an increase in acidity of more than 100 times. The pH of Loch Skerrow has dropped from 6.8 to 5.7 since 1961; that of Loch Garroch from 6.6 to 4.9. Most of the acidification has taken place on the parts of Galloway that are underlain by granite. The old volcanic rock is hard and resists erosion. So it yields few chemicals that might neutralize acid. But even on more yielding rocks there have been some similar changes. Loch Harrow had a pH of 6.3 in 1953. It is 5.4 today. Nearby Loch Minnoch had a pH of 6.1 in 1953. It is 5.3 today.

Rivers draining north and south from the Galloway hills, such as the Cree and Bladnock, are also becoming acid and recent surveys have found trout to be very rare or absent in many Galloway streams. The pH of the Cree is down to 4.5 during the egg-hatching season. Local pollution inspectors say this   is likely to be 'very serious for eggs'. The Clyde River Purification Board has pinpointed 'a sharp fall' in the mean pH of Loch Doon in the north Galloway hills since 1983.[11] It fell to 4.5 in 1985.

Scientists from University College in London have investigated the skeletons of tiny algae that have lived and died in the Scottish lochs for thousands of years. The organisms, called diatoms, are extremely sensitive to acid and, depending on the precise acidity of the water in which they live, one species or another of diatoms will dominate. So their skeletons, laid down in layers in the loch's sediment, provide a history of the acidification of a loch for anyone with a microscope and an ability to count. Rick Battarbee and his colleagues have discovered how sudden, abrupt and unprecedented the recent acidification of the lochs has been.[12] The discovery has made Battarbee and his small band of diatomists into some of the hottest properties in the acid-rain industry, showered with offers of grant money for their research.

Of six Galloway lochs investigated, Battarbee has found recent acidification in five. At Loch Enoch, the pH of the water remained stable at about 5.2 between 1600 and 1840. Then the acidification began, accelerating to a peak in the 1930s and stabilizing in the mid-1970s with the pH down to 4.3. The Round Loch of Grannoch kept a steady pH of more than 5.5 until 1850. Since then it has declined to 4.8. Loch Grannoch started to acidify in the 1930s.

Battarbee's team has found that particles of soot and heavy metals appear among the diatom skeletons in the sediment laid down since the mid-nineteenth century. This seems a clear sign that air pollution triggered the acidification of the lochs of Galloway. Battarbee says he can find no evidence of any change in land use that might have affected the lochs as they start to turn acid.

For a while it seemed as if the acidification of Galloway might be unique in Britain. But the more scientists have looked, the more evidence of acid waters and declining fish stocks they have found elsewhere. The Isle of Arran has some of the most acid rivers and lochs in west Scotland. The island is in the Firth of Clyde and would have felt the earliest effects of the industrialization of Glasgow. Iorsa Water is the island's longest river. The Clyde River Purification Board has found that 'salmon were apparently abundant in the Iorsa in the late eighteenth century, but by 1840 stocks had declined noticeably.'[13] By the 1950s, there were 'a few sea trout and an occasional salmon'. Today, yields have improved. But only because the acid upper reaches of the river have been bypassed by the planting out of salmon ova lower down the river. The rivers of north Argyll around Oban are acid. So are several streams and lochs on the island of Jura. And two Islay lochs have a pH as low as 3.9. Fish have died in the rver Ba on the island of Mull. In February 1984, an extensive loss of fish occurred in the western Highlands – on the same day as black snow fell in the Cairngorms.

Acid pulses caused by severe downpours of acid rain are a constant threat to fish in many parts of Scotland. The East Kilbride weather station recorded a rainstorm with a pH of 2.8 in 1983. One day in March 1984 accounted for 9 per cent of all the acid fallout at the station that year.[14] Many streams in Scotland, especially in granite areas, carry very little calcium to neutralize these acid pulses. And that is one reason why experts are holding their breath for the future of fishing on the Balmoral estate – the vast Scottish retreat of the royal family that spreads across the most vulnerable territory in the heart of the Cairngorm mountains.

There is growing concern that the lochs and streams of the Cairngorms face a fate as severe as that of the waters of Galloway. The North East River Purification Board drew up a list in 1983 of well-fished waters in its area that would be extremely vulnerable to an acid pulse. Most were in the upper reaches of the Spey and Dee catchments, draining the heart of the Cairngorms.[15] Top of the list was Loch Muick on the edge of Balmoral forest. Several lochs on the estate are already fishless. Lochnager, made famous by Prince Charles in his book for children, *The Old Man of Lochnagaer*, has an average pH of 4.9.[16] At last count, thirteen trout survived in this loch. But scientists working in the area, such as Trevor Davies of the University of East Anglia, say that acid pulses during snowmelts could kill off the fish in many such lochs on high ground in the Cairngorms. The royal family may soon have to look beyond Balmoral for its fishing expeditions.

The evidence is growing that something nasty may be happening in the Lake District of England – especially in the west, in rivers draining Sca Fell. Concern began in 1980 when more than a hundred adult trout and salmon and many more young fish were found dead in the catchment of the river Esk in south-west Cumbria. North West Water, which has a legal duty to look after fish stocks on its patch, investigated. Its scientists reported in 1984 that in both the

Esk and the Duddon catchments there were 'a number of surface waters from which fish appear to have vanished within the last ten to fifteen years'.[17]

Notebooks kept by local anglers show that fish were regularly caught in the River Esk at Great Moss up to 1965. No fish were found there during surveys in 1980 and 1981. At Lincove Beck and Spothow Hill, fish were caught in 1970, but recent surveys have found none. In Levers Water, which is used by the water authority as a reservoir, fish were found in 1975. But today there are no fish in the reservoir or in the streams that feed it.

Some of the problem in the lower reaches might be connected with farming. But in the higher streams where the salmon spawn, this is unlikely. The authority's scientists say the fish are being killed by toxic aluminium washed out of the soils by acid waters. They say: 'It is clear that the water quality of the Esk is at best only just capable of supporting viable fish populations.' Any upset can tip it over the edge. One local biologist describes the lakes as having a 'highly nervous system'.[18]

Heavy rain after a dry spell is especially dangerous. In a survey of upland tarns (small lakes), fifteen showed a sudden drop in pH in January 1984 after snowfall. In one, Blea Tarn, the pH fell from 6.0 to 4.1 – almost a hundredfold increase in acidity. Many of the tarns did not recover until May. Earlier that winter, there had been another serious loss of fish in the Esk catchment.[17]

The traditional view has been that the acid lakes and rivers of west Cumbria and much of the rest of highland Britain have been acid for perhaps 5,000 years.[19] At that time, Neolithic men chopped down the ancient forests of highland Britain. Heathland and peat bogs formed. Biologists have until recently assumed that the lakes and rivers would have turned acid at the same times as the soils. It seemed a reasonable assumption. But it is probably wrong.

Rick Battarbee's diatomists have extended their analysis of the sediment of the Round Loch of Grannoch in Galloway back to 9,000 years ago. In mid-1986, they reported that the development of acid soils and later formation of blanket peat in the catchment of the Round Loch around 5,000 years ago had no influence on loch acidity.[20] The pH of the loch stayed between 5.5 and 6.0 right up until 1850, when it fell in a few decades to 4.7. 'We conclude,' they said, 'that soil acidification is not the likely cause of the very low pH values found in many acidified lakes today.' This finding shocked a lot of scientists in the field. And, if repeated at other sites, it could have important implications, not least for the Lake District.

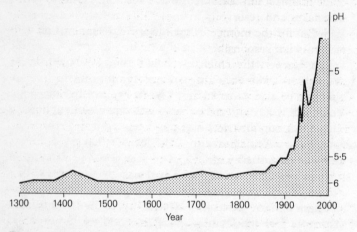

Reconstructed acidity of Round Loch in Galloway, as revealed by diatom analysis.

J. F. Robinson from North West Water reached a similar conclusion from his work in the Lake District. He found that 'the most peaty streams were also the least acid . . . It seems unlikely that organic acids derived from peat are making a significant contribution to the acidity of these streams.' It is acid rain, and especially the sulphate ion in the rain, that does the damage.

Scientists from the Freshwater Biological Association based in Windermere have recently investigated diatoms beneath Scoat Tarn, a tiny lake perched 700 metres up, between Ennerdale and Wastwater.[18] There seems to have been a reduction in the pH of the tarn of at least one unit (implying a tenfold increase in acidity) since 1850. And it was still becoming more acid at least as recently as 1950. The evidence is growing that acid rain, and especially the sulphate ion in the rain, is responsible for much more of the acid in highland lakes and rivers than has previously been supposed.

Since the start of the Industrial Revolution, air pollution has done severe ecological damage to the southern Pennines. It killed the bog moss that created the extensive peat beds, and made it almost impossible for many species of trees to grow. The lakes and reservoirs in these hills are often extremely acid. But for the moment, the official view remains that acid fallout is not responsible.

Eric Harper, the chief scientific officer for North West Water, says: 'We have always tended to assume . . . the attribution of acidity to "natural" acidity from Pennine soils.' Yorkshire Water says the same. As we have seen in Galloway and the Lake District, there is no justification for this assumption. Acid, peaty soils do not by themselves create acid waters. A survey of seventy-two lakes and pools in three separate moorland areas in Britain found twenty-nine with a pH of less than 4.4. Of these, twenty-three were in the southern Pennines. Near Huddersfield and Sheffield, biologists have found pH values as low as 3.0 in moorland pools. It seems that areas with high amounts of acid fallout have acid waters. Such areas either have high rainfall (such as the Lake District) or are close to industrial areas (such as the southern Pennines). Peaty areas with lower acid inputs have much less acid waters.

Data from North West Water's reservoirs provide more evidence. Peaty soils are found throughout the authority's region, which extends from the southern Pennines to the Lake District. Yet only fifteen of the authority's reservoirs have an average pH of less than 5. All but one of these is within forty kilometres of Manchester, in a narrow arc downwind, north and east of the city. The most acid of these is the Warland reservoir, midway between Rochdale and Halifax, in an exposed rainy spot more than 300 metres up. It has an average pH of 3.6 and a minimum in a typical year

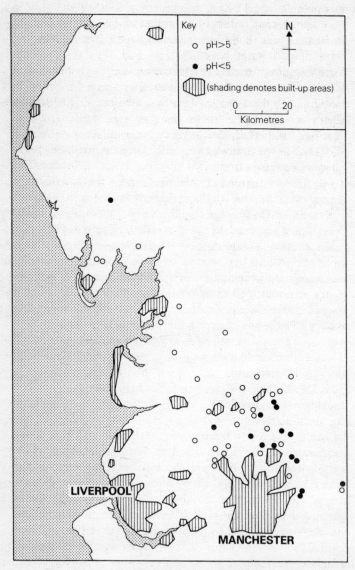

The pH of water in reservoirs run by North West Water.

of 3.2. Two reservoirs with a pH of 4.0 are at Wickenhall, on moorland between Rochdale and Oldham, and at Swineshaw, just outside Stalybridge.

A 25-per-cent reduction in emissions of sulphur dioxide in Britain since 1980 has set many researchers looking for signs of acid water becoming less acid. The reservoirs of Yorkshire are providing the first evidence of a change. There are three reservoirs in the Calder valley west of Halifax. At Hollins Hall, the average pH of samples taken by Yorkshire Water rose from 4.2 in the late 1970s to 4.7 in 1985. At nearby Thrum Hall, the average rose from 4.6 to 6.1 and at Withens Clough from 4.2 to 4.6. In the same area, the pH at Gorpley has risen from 4.5 to 5.7 and at Holmebridge from 4.5 to 5.1.[21] The trend is strong evidence that acid fallout is an important reason why these reservoirs are acid.

The salmon of Wales are dying out. A study by Welsh Water, published in late 1985, reported 'an obvious and generally marked decline in the total number of salmon caught by both rod and net on almost every river system'.[22] The report blamed poaching and the increasing acidity of Welsh rivers. It underlined the growing concern of Welsh Water's scientists about the principality's acid waters. In September 1984 more than a hundred sea trout and many other fish were found dead on the banks of the Afon Glaslyn in north Wales. The fish had died from poisoning by acid and the aluminium that it had washed into the river.

Roscoe Howells, Welsh Water's director of scientific services, says: 'It is likely that the upper reaches of most of Wales' salmon and sea-trout rivers may be affected by acidification.' In fifteen lakes around Blaenau Ffestiniog in Snowdonia, including Gamallt Faw, Gammalt Fach and Llyn Conwy, 'severe declines in brown trout recruitment are associated with acid water. The Berwyn catchment in north Wales is now too acidic to support the American brook char, which was introduced to cope with the acid,' he says. At Llyn Conwy the pH is down to 4.6. A few large, old trout are all that survive in the two Gammalt lakes, as breeding has ceased.

In one study, Howells' scientists set out to investigate why salmon and trout in two neighbouring streams in central

Wales had disappeared.[23] They 'planted' a thousand salmon in the rivers Tywi and Camddwr. When they went back two months later, the salmon were gone. Later studies found that the average survival time for salmon was thirteen days in the Tywi and eighteen days in the Camddwr. The gills of the dead fish contained massive amounts of aluminium.

The Freshwater Biological Association conducted a fish count in the rivers Wye and Severn in 1979. It found a 'much reduced population of brown trout'.[24] Severn Trent Water has investigated the pH of the river Severn, which supplies much of the West Midlands with water. It found that at Caersws in the Welsh hills there had been a threefold increase in acidity since 1975. Further upstream at Llanidloes, the pH of the river's water had slipped into the 'danger area' for fish of between 6 and 6.5. In 1975, only 5 per cent of samples of the river's water had a pH as low as this. By 1983, 30 per cent did.[25] Altogether, more than a third of Wales is now drained by streams with a pH of less than 5.5.

'It is always raining up here,' says Steve Ormerod. We are driving, in a Welsh Water van, on the winding road that threads its way round Llyn Brianne, a reservoir high in the hills of central Wales. The roads are deserted except for sheep and the occasional lorry carrying timber cut down by the Forestry Commission. On our left, 60,000 hectares of moorland has been preserved for raven, merlin and other birds of prey. But in recent years much of the rest has been turned over to Sitka spruce, Lodgepole pine and Japanese larch.

As European rain goes, Welsh rain is not very acid. Most of it comes in off the Atlantic Ocean, and the average pH is around 4.7. But on the hilltops it is more acid, and when the wind is from England the pH can get down to 3.8. The soils are thin and Ormerod and his colleagues from Welsh Water have become convinced that the forestry plantations are helping to convert the moderately acid rain into a brew that kills fish. The land that surrounds Llyn Brianne has become the scene of the most sophisticated attempt yet to establish the role of forests in helping acidify streams and lakes.

The mass of tiny streams that drain into Llyn Brianne will

each have a particular role in the experiment. Somewhere along each stream there is a green box, about the size of a phone box, that contains equipment for measuring the flow and chemistry of the stream every fifteen minutes.

There are several questions to answer. How good is the foliage of trees at catching acid in passing clouds? Do the trees remove important neutralizing chemicals such as calcium from the soil? Do drains, dug to stop the trees becoming waterlogged, speed the runoff of acid rain into streams? If they do, this would cut the amount of time the soil has to neutralize the acid rain.

To test such theories, one catchment will have drains dug, but no trees planted; another forested area will be 'bombed' with lime to neutralize any acid; others will be ploughed up or have fertilizers put on them; still others, both forested and bare, will be left alone. The green boxes will then monitor the results.

The work might relieve acid rain of some blame for killing fish. But the Welsh scientists say that without acid rain there would probably be no problem. It is the combination of acid rain and trees that seems to be lethal here. And they warn that plans by the foresters to double the number of trees in upland Britain by the year 2,000 makes it imperative to find out the trees' true role.

The most vulnerable waters in Wales, Llyn Conwy and its neighbours, and the streams of Snowdonia have become acid without a tree being planted near them. This echoes Battarbee's work in Galloway, which has found no link between tree planting and acid lakes. But in marginal areas, conifer plantations seem to be able to tip the balance. In a major study of acid streams in the large catchment of the rivers Wye and Irfon, Ormerod found 'a decline in measured pH at all sites' between the late 1960s and the mid 1980s.[26] The decline averaged 1.7 pH units in forested areas and 0.7 units on bare moorland.

Today, nowhere seems safe from acid rain. In Northern Ireland, government biologists have found an area of acid waters in the Mourn mountains, including reservoirs such as the Silent Valley and Ben Crom reservoirs, which are permanently acid.[27] And it reports vulnerable areas around the Sperrin and North Antrim hills. The pH of the river Annalong falls as low as 4.3.

Acid rain is hitting south-east England. The Ashdown forest in Sussex is one of the ancient commonlands of England and source of the river Medway and the Sussex Ouse. The soil is sandstone and the waters are acid. Alan Hildrew from Queen Mary College, London took part in a study of thirty-four sites along streams in the forest. More than half sometimes had a pH of 5 or below.[28] The minimum, recorded on a tributary of the Medway, was 3.6. Hildrew concludes that acid rain was partly responsible. 'The soils of the catchment are themselves poor and sandy with little buffering capacity against the increasingly acid rainfall,' he says.

The more acid streams of the Ashdown forest have lost their brown trout and have fewer invertebrate animals on the stream bottoms than the less acid streams. Fragmentary findings of a similar nature have come from other researchers, notably those working for the government's Nature Conservancy Council.[29] Newts seem to be becoming scarce in the New Forest in Hampshire, an area where there is some evidence of streams becoming more acid in the past decade. Natterjack toads do not breed successfully in water with a pH of less than 6 and the council reports that they have 'disappeared from many parts of Britain, especially from east and south-east England. Some breeding pools on heathland appear to have become more acidic over the last forty years; acid deposition might be implicated.'

Back in Wales, Steve Ormerod takes time off from measuring the chemistry of streams for Welsh Water to count dipper birds for the Royal Society for the Protection of Birds. These extraordinary birds swim and walk under water in search of insect larvae. Acid waters contain fewer insects and the dippers are disappearing from acid rivers such as the Wye in mid-Wales, while thriving in rivers that have not gone acid. 'The distribution of dippers can be correlated with stream acidity,' says Ormerod.[30]

These examples may be the tip of a very large iceberg. We do not know. There is great potential for damage to wildlife of all sorts from acid rain. As the Nature Conservancy Council reports: 'There are now many national nature reserves and sites of special scientific interest . . . exposed to acid deposition.' Of 357 sites listed by the Nature Conservancy Council as being of international importance for nature conservation, more than a hundred are in areas with geology that is especially vulnerable to acidification.

What hope is there for recovery? There are a few hopeful signs – notably in the Yorkshire Pennines where, as we have seen, the pH has risen dramatically in several reservoirs close to industrial towns. But for more remote locations Britain's scientists are pessimistic. Many of them have contributed to the development of a detailed theoretical model of how acid rain makes lakes and streams acid. It takes account of such things as forest planting and the ability of various soils to both store and neutralize acid. The model, known as MAGIC, predicts that in places such as Galloway a continuation of current levels of acid fallout will mean that 'annual average stream pH is likely to continue to decline'. Even a 50 per cent cut in deposition between 1984 and the year 2000 would, the model suggests, only be sufficient to stabilize acidity at the current levels.[31]

Liming: The Quick Fix

The first lakes in Europe to be made acid by air pollution were in Britain – probably in the Lake District and the southern Pennines. The next were in Norway. Then came Sweden. Lake Gardsjon is in the mountains on the southwest coast of Sweden. Until Swedish scientists descended on it in the 1970s, it was typical of Sweden's 'problem' lakes.

Hans Hultberg from the Swedish Environmental Research Institute has been involved in studies of the lake from the beginning.[32] 'Lake Gardsjon and other neighbouring lakes have seen fish decline since the late 1940s,' he says. 'It became a major problem during the 1960s.' From 1900, when records began, to the 1960s there had been healthy populations of perch, roach, pike and eel in the lake. But by 1973, only forty-seven perch were left.

The history of Lake Gardsjon's acidification is revealed by studies of diatoms in the lake's sediment that go back to 12,500 BC, the date when the ice sheets of the last glaciation finally retreated from south-west Sweden. The story is familiar. Between 12,500 BC and AD 1950, the pH of the waters gradually subsided, as a result of natural processes, from around 7 to around 6. 'After 1950,' says Hultberg, 'a rapid acidification from pH 6.0 to 4.7 has occurred.'

First, acid surges occurred during snowmelt and the first rains of autumn. Then the lake became acid all year. In the early 1980s, as sulphur emissions began to decline in western Europe, the amount of sulphur in the lake dropped by about 20 per cent. But, says Hultberg, 'nitrate levels increased as nitrate emissions rose in Europe.'

Sweden, like Norway, is a nation of fishermen. It has 85,000 lakes. Nearly a quarter of them, 18,000 in all, have been acidified: most of them, according to the government's Environmental Protection Board, as a result of acid rain.[33] Of these, half, or 9,000 lakes, have suffered losses to their fish stocks. So too have many of the important salmon rivers. Like Norway, the fish losses are heavily concentrated on the thin-soiled mountainous terrain of the far south of the country, where westerly and southerly winds bring pollution. According to the Environmental Protection Board the sulphur fallout in acid rain 'needs to be reduced by 70 to 80 per cent in southern Sweden, if all the low-buffered waters are to be protected'.

Acid lakes and rivers have been seen, until recently, as an exclusively Scandinavian problem. Now Britain is being shown to suffer. But Dick Wright, the campaigning American at the Norwegian Institute for Water Research, believes that the phenomenon affects nearly every country in Europe.

Wright identifies three kinds of soils where acid fallout may turn rivers and lakes acid.[34] There are the thin soils of Scandinavia and Scotland, where the underlying granite rocks provide little material to neutralize acid. There are sandy soils, found in Denmark, the Low Countries and parts of lowland England. These too have little power to neutralize acid. And there are the soils of central Europe where massive acid fallout has overrun better-developed natural defences, turning soils acid and moving on into rivers.

As a rule of thumb, Wright says that rain with a pH of less than 4.7 is likely to acidify lakes. So most of Europe from the Alps north is at risk, except Ireland, western France, northern Norway and Sweden – and most of Finland. In southern Finland, where the rain is acid, diatomists have found lakes that have acidified in the past thirty years.

Diatoms show that lakes in prized Danish nature reserves, such as the Lobelia lakes of central Jutland and the tiny dune lakes of north-west Jutland, have been disrupted by acid rain. And streams on sandy soils in lowland England have also become more acid in recent years. There are similar reports from moorland pools in the Netherlands and Belgium.

In central Europe the more mature, richer soils do not readily pass acid on to streams. This only happens after the soils themselves have become acid, which frequently means that forest damage appears first. Areas where this has happened include the Harz mountains in Lower Saxony, Schilitzerlandse in Hessen, the Thuringerwald of East Germany and the Erzgebirge on the dreadfully polluted border between East Germany and Czechoslovakia. In the forests of Bavaria, diatomists have found lakes that have become ten times more acid in the past thirty years.

Wright says lakes in many more areas have yet to be investigated. These include 'the Vosges mountains and Massif Central in France, the Alps of both Switzerland and Austria, the Schwarzwald in West Germany and the Tatry mountains of Czechoslovakia'.

In the short term, the only way to save acid lakes for fish is to dump lime in them to neutralize acid. In the first half of the 1980s, Sweden sprayed almost a million tonnes of finely ground limestone into about 3,000 lakes. It has cost around $30 million. Norway has tried it. So too has Welsh Water in lakes near Aberystwyth. And the Central Electricity Generating Board is chartering helicopters to spray lime on to the soil around Loch Fleet in the Galloway hills of Scotland.

The board says, 'a European fund to pay for liming would

involve less than one-hundredth the cost of the programme of sulphur dioxide controls being proposed.'[35] Maybe so, but its own scientists admit that they do not expect to be able to bring natural fisheries back to Loch Fleet however much lime they put into the loch. This is because the tiny streams that feed the loch are virtually impossible to dose effectively and will stay acid. It is in the streams that the fish spawn.

The Norwegians say that comprehensive liming of lakes would be a massive, permanent exercise involving fleets of helicopters roaming the hills. Many of the most acid lakes are in places where there are no roads. And the technology to dose running rivers is still not sufficiently developed.

While liming can get rid of acid in lakes, it does not get rid of the toxic aluminium liberated from the soils by acid rain. The aluminium is converted by the lime into a sediment of aluminium hydroxide that builds up on the bed of the lake. Should the liming ever stop, that accumulated aluminium would reconvert to its toxic form and redissolve into the water.

Liming lakes and streams is no long-term solution, as the CEGB now agrees. But liming soils is likely to be an essential component of any strategy to clean up the massive accumulations of acid and sulphur left in soils by decades of acid fallout. Even if all the man-made emissions of acid in Europe were switched off tomorrow, accumulated sulphate and acid would continue to pour out of soils for years, perhaps decades, to come. The acid must be neutralized and the sulphur fixed in the soil, and that will require massive amounts of limestone spread on soils all over Scandinavia.

Acid on Tap

Acid water can maim babies – sometimes before they are born. It kills fish by poisoning them with aluminium. It harms babies by giving them and their mothers lead. If the lead does not kill the foetus, it may damage the development of the nervous system of young children, making them less intelligent and more violent, nervous and moody.

For babies, as for fish, the risks are high in Scotland. Here, millions of people live in areas where the public water supply comes from reservoirs where the water is soft and acid, partly because of acid rain. This water scours the lead from the old lead pipes and tanks that are still found in millions of homes in Scotland and all over Britain. The lead, in a highly digestible form, comes out of the tap.

Since the late 1970s, the fear that babies and young children are being poisoned by lead from tap-water has been one of the biggest worries of the British government's health advisers. They believe lead from tap-water is a far greater risk than lead from petrol exhausts. In March 1981 Sir Henry Yellowlees, the government's chief medical officer, warned ministers that lead pollution might be damaging the nervous systems of 'some hundreds of thousands of children'.[36]

Many towns now add lime to their water to reduce the acidity and so stop it dissolving lead. To comply with a directive from the European Community, the British government has set a deadline of 1990 for the completion of this task. Even then, thousands of small private water supplies will remain potentially lethal.

The most devastating evidence about the scale of the problem was 'presented to parliament' in 1980. Actually, a report was placed in the House of Commons library late one Friday afternoon just before Christmas. The study, by the Greater Glasgow Health Board, revealed that more than a tenth of all new-born babies in Glasgow entered the world with more lead in their blood than is considered safe for adults.[37] This happens because lead drunk by a pregnant mother crosses the placenta and accumulates in the body of her foetus. Five per cent of mothers in the survey had more than the international limit of 350 micrograms of lead in every litre of blood in their bodies. Eleven per cent of their new-born babies exceeded the limit.

The report followed a series of startling discoveries by Glasgow doctors during the late 1970s about the harm that lead was doing to Glaswegian children. A leading figure in these investigations was Dr Michael Moore of the University of Glasgow. He found that Glaswegian foetuses whose mothers drank water with a high lead content were twice as likely to be mentally retarded.[38] They were also more likely to be born early or to be stillborn. Scientists measured the amount of lead in the placenta of mothers of normal babies and of mothers whose babies were either stillborn or died shortly after birth. Among the normal babies, only 7 per cent of placentae had lead levels greater than 1.5 parts per million. Where things had gone wrong, 61 per cent had high lead levels.[39] Moore says that nowhere in Europe has suffered as badly from lead poisoning as Glasgow and the west of Scotland.

Glasgow's water comes from Loch Katrine, a large natural reservoir about fifty kilometres north of the city on the edge of the Scottish highlands. Its catchment has taken the brunt of pollution from Glaswegian industry for a century or more. The pH of the loch, at 6.3, is not extreme by Scottish standards. But the water is very soft, having only a thirtieth as much calcium as London water. It is very good at dissolving lead.[40]

As the Glaswegian doctors began to uncover an epidemic of lead poisoning in their city, American studies found that 'children with high lead levels were three times more likely to have an IQ below 80 points [that is, they were fairly dim]'.[41] Teachers said that those children were also much less attentive in class.

A later study of adult American workers in a lead works found that those with the most lead in their blood were more moody, had worse memories, and had difficulty with language and responding to visual signals. After lead pollution at the factory was cleaned up, the same men showed less anger, tension, depression, fatigue and confusion.[42]

Alerted to the dangers, Scottish doctors began to find more and more cases of children poisoned by lead from tap-water. A fifth of mothers and babies in Ayr, down the coast from Glasgow, had more than 350 micrograms of lead in each litre of their blood. Lead in tap-water was up to twenty times the international limit. The highest figures were found in a school. Acid waters from two lochs that fed the town's taps, Loch Finlas and Loch Recawr, were blamed. Mothers of all babies in the town under six months old were given bottles of distilled water from which to make up their babies' feed. Altogether, more than 400 water sources in the Strathclyde region around Glasgow were identified as potentially dangerous. In Glasgow, three-quarters of houses over twenty years old, most of which would have had lead pipes, had levels of lead in their water that were unsafe.

Britain's water authorities have told ministers that five million people live in areas where tap-water may contain excessive amounts of lead.[43] Ministers say that by 1990 all those people will be protected by the dosing of vulnerable acid waters with lime. The aim is to ensure that water throughout the national distribution network does not fall below a pH of 8. That is less than the 8.5 that the water industry's scientists said was 'optimal'. But, even so, can the target be met? Some Scottish engineers who have tried it are doubtful. In Ayr, they lifted the pH at the treatment works to 8.7, but at the tap it was often as low as 7.6. That is a lot better than the pH of 6 sometimes found before, but the town's environmental health officers admit that there are still problems.

In north-west England, 600,000 houses are served by long, communal lead pipes. Soft, acid water from moorland reservoirs may sit for hours or even days in these pipes before reaching the tap, dissolving lead all the while.

There are hundreds of thousands more people in Britain who are not connected to the public mains and receive private water supplies. In Scotland and Wales, that often means water straight off the hillside from tiny reservoirs serving a few houses. Such supplies are almost impossible to dose efficiently with lime, agrees Robert Little, the environmental-health officer for Tweeddale in the Scottish border country. Outside Peebles, he says, almost all the houses in his district receive water that dissolves lead. Most, he says, fail the European Community directive. There are so many small, private water supplies that Little does not even have plans to take water samples from them all, let alone ensure that they are safe. In many parts of the district, he says, farms and estate buildings have lead-lined tanks and lead plumbing. There can be no doubt that this is extremely dangerous.

Scotland has the highest death rate from heart disease in

the world. It seems that the soft, acid waters that come out of most of the nation's taps may be partly to blame, though nobody is quite sure why. It could be lead or some other metal absorbed by the acid water. It could be its softness, that is, the absence of nutrient chemicals such as calcium or magnesium. Or it could be a mixture of the two. If so, it is strikingly similar to the reason for the death in acid waters of fish (too much metallic aluminium and too little calcium) and trees in acid soils (too little magnesium and too much aluminium).

People who live around Glasgow are more than twice as likely to die of heart disease as those who live in towns around London. The ten-year-old British Regional Heart Study is designed to find out why. Part of the reason is that the Scots are poorer, smoke more and have a cold, damp climate. But after allowing for a mass of such factors, the scientists running the study say that 10 to 15 per cent of heart disease is inextricably connected to soft, acid tap-water.[44] Ayr and Kilmarnock in Scotland, and Halifax and Dewsbury in Yorkshire are towns where the effect of acid water is especially marked. We have already seen how acid water in Ayr has caused lead poisoning among the town's children. Halifax and Dewsbury get their water from reservoirs in the Pennines, where massive acid pollution began with the Industrial Revolution.

The British deaths from heart disease that are linked to soft, acid water number between 5,000 and 8,000 every year. People in 'acid towns' also suffer from high blood pressure. It is, says Professor Gerry Shaper, one of the study's coordinators, 'almost like the difference between two nations'.

Early investigations in Scotland suggested that lead was the link between soft, acid water and heart disease. Such a link is clear for animals, and French and American scientists have reached the same conclusions for humans. One major American study found that if lead in blood could be cut by a third, heart failure could be cut by 5 per cent and strokes by 7 per cent.[45] But the British Regional Heart Study, which has homed in on middle-aged men, who are most at risk of heart disease, does not confirm this.[46]

Attention has turned to the absence of calcium in soft, acid water. As we have seen, acid rain gradually consumes calcium in soils and waters. Calcium is as important a nutrient for humans as it is for fish and trees. It also has an important relationship with lead and other toxic metals. In most living organisms, the good things of life – such as calcium and magnesium – follow similar metabolic pathways to the bad things – toxic elements such as lead and aluminium. Aluminium invades tree roots when there is not enough calcium or magnesium around. Lead invades human bodies, coursing through veins and turning up in bones and teeth, if there is not enough calcium around. So the truth may be that the absence of the beneficial elements, and the presence of the toxic elements in acid water, are both important in causing heart disease.

Aluminium can kill trees when soils turn acid. And if acid rain washes the metal from soils into streams, it kills fish. If that water collects in a reservoir, the aluminium gets drunk by people, too. The question is: does it do them harm as well?

Doctors know that in extreme cases aluminium does kill people. Sheila Brayford from Staffordshire died in 1981 from brain damage caused by absorbing aluminium into her bloodstream during kidney dialysis. During treatment, kidney patients are exposed to pullutants in hundreds of litres of water used in the process. When Sheila Brayford died, she had a hundred times the normal amount of aluminium in her body.

The brains of dialysis patients are exceptionally vulnerable to aluminium in water. But other people may be at risk too. Scientists from the Medical Research Council reported early in 1986 on growing evidence that aluminium 'may be involved in the initiation or early stages' of Alzheimer's Disease, a virulent form of senile dementia that is a growing scourge of the old.[47] In the USA, similar suspicions have been aroused, especially after the discovery that inhabitants in remote islands with soils rich in aluminium-containing bauxite, such as Guam and west New Guinea, suffer a similar disease.[48] In the USA the disease is now the fourth-biggest killer among the elderly, claiming 120,000 lives every year.

Doctors are finding high concentrations of aluminium right at the place where the two classic symptoms of the disease occur. These features are known as neurofibrillary tangles, clumps of twisted nerve-cell fibres in the brain, and senile plaques, knobby patches of dying nerve fibres. The doctors said: 'this accumulation is thought to be consequent to . . . an environment low in calcium and magnesium and rich in aluminium.'

Water is a principal source of aluminium in the human body. It is less important than food, but scientists investigating its role warn that they are still very uncertain about which forms of the metal are most toxic, and which turn up in food and water. It may be that the toxic forms predominate in acid waters. Nobody knows. But, for many scientists, the dead fish in aluminium-poisoned streams and lakes from Norway to Wales are a clear warning. Aluminium in acid water seems to be specially dangerous. And late in 1986, Norwegian researchers published the first evidence that there are significantly more cases of Alzheimer's Disease in the Southern countries of Norway, where there is more aluminium in the lakes, and the most acid rain.

A directive from the European Community limits the amount of aluminium in tap-water. The long list of towns in England that exceed that limit is a catalogue of those places hit by acid waters.[49] It includes the parts of Birmingham and the West Midlands that take their water from the acid headwaters of the River Severn in Wales; communities clustered around Manchester, and Yorkshire towns such as Sheffield, Huddersfield and Bradford.

4 The Strange Death of Europe's Trees

Waldsterben, a German Catastrophe

From the autobahns it is often not easy to believe that Germany's trees are sick. There are few skeletons of dead trees silhouetted against the sky. But take a plane and look down in search of the familiar mat of green foliage that until recently covered almost a third of the country. Instead, you see that the upper surfaces of the needles of billions of trees have turned a sickly yellow. From the Harz mountains of Lower Saxony to the Black Forest and the Alps – everywhere you see the same thing. These yellow needles, rarely seen before, are the 'new disease' of German trees. They call it *Waldsterben*. The disease seems to be quite different from the lethal assault by high concentrations of sulphur dioxide that still occurs in parts of Eastern Europe. It is more subtle and more difficult to explain. But it is spreading fast, all over western Europe.

The forests are the traditional playground for Germans. They drive their Mercedes, Audis and BMWs into the woods to marvel at nature in the midst of their modern world. But the factories that make their wealth, and the cars that are such a feature of their affluence, are killing the trees.

The foresters, an esteemed fraternity in Germany, say that more than half of the nation's trees are damaged by *Waldsterben* – a fifth of them seriously. They all agree that air pollution is to blame. Outside Nuremberg in Bavaria they have fenced off a stand of trees and marked the health of each tree from one to five. A sign tells visitors: 'These trees have been damaged by sulphur dioxide from industrial pollution.'

In retrospect, the first signs of trouble were there in the

late 1970s. But when Bernhardt Ulrich made awful predictions of decline in 1981, foresters gave him a cool reception. Until that year the damage had been sporadic. But by 1983, 34 per cent of German trees were reported to be sick. And in 1984 the proportion had reached 50 per cent, a level that has persisted since. The disease has been most devastating among Norway spruce, which account for almost half of all German trees.

Any forester would expect some sickness among his trees. Part of the explanation for the soaring percentages may be that foresters have learned better how to see the dead wood for the trees. But even British doubters who visited Germany in 1984 were convinced. Bill Binns of the Forestry Commission says he was shocked by the decline in the two years since his previous visit. Damage that had started on mountaintops in the Black Forest was spreading inexorably down the mountainsides. Foresters in the Black Forest had earmarked a stand of trees that they monitored in detail each year. In 1980, none of the 500 spruce trees in the stand showed visible damage. But by 1983 all showed some signs of decline and three-quarters showed serious yellowing or loss of needles.

During a trip round West Germany in March 1986 I met no German forester or scientist who did not believe that air pollution was the underlying cause of the epidemic. However, they all agreed that the weather, especially the hot, dry summers in 1982 and 1983, had put extra stress on weakened trees and may have triggered the catastrophe. Trees weakened by pollution could not extract from the parched soil the moisture and nutrient chemicals that they needed to survive. Magnesium, which is in short supply in many German soils, became deficient in the trees first. When the deficiency reached the needles, they turned yellow. The very wet summers of 1984 and 1985 allowed a brief respite in the decline. But nobody is saying that the worst is over. Some foresters agree with Ulrich that virtually no young trees in West Germany today will reach maturity.

There is a certain bravado about the scientists from Bayreuth University in Bavaria. They are within spitting distance

Waldsterben in West Germany, 1985

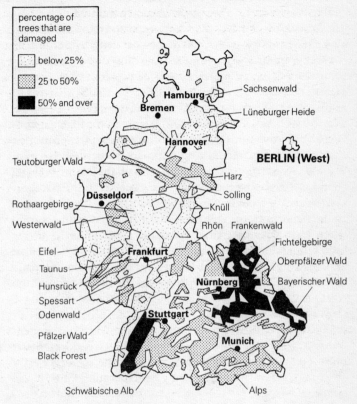

Damage diagram of German forests

of the Iron Curtain and drive past a well-fortified American listening post on their way to see some of the most damaged stands of trees in the local Fichtelgebirge mountains. Yet they drive a red Russian 'jeep'. In the jeep are Kenneth Werk, a Canadian, and Ram Oren, an Israeli. Both have been poached from American universities by their cosmopolitan professor, Ernst-Detlef Schulze. Snow blocks the road at Schneberg, a hilltop close to the listening station. The trees there are all dead. Down the surrounding hillside, the spruce are stunted; many are blown down and have been dragged away by foresters. In the winter mist it is an eerie scene. 'This is our moonscape,' says Oren.

There are, according to those who have counted, 186 scientific hypotheses for what has happened to trees here and all over Germany. Nobody at Bayreuth is about to add to the confusion by offering another. 'The trouble,' says Oren as we head up a mountain track, 'is that everybody wants their own hypothesis, but nobody wants to do the hard sweat of testing their hypothesis in the field.' Ten minutes later, the two researchers are clambering through metre-high snow to fiddle with tiny electrodes stuck into the bark of a spruce tree and to lug heavy monitoring equipment back to the jeep. They have two open-air laboratories high in the Fichtelgebirge. These stations are at the heart of the first comprehensive German investigation of what is really happening to the nation's trees. It involves twenty-three institutions at seven Bavarian universities, but is almost unknown on the international acid-rain conference-circuit. Most German biologists have too many conference suits and too few pairs of gumboots. At Bayreuth they stay at home and do the research.

'It's a shame what the acid-rain debate has done to certain scientists,' says Schulze. One heavily publicized proponent of the idea that viruses are killing the trees has never published the results of any research on the subject. So far as anybody knows, he has not actually found his virus, either.

So, what exactly is going on in the German forests? There are two main theories about how air pollution is damaging the trees. They are the bottom-up hypothesis and the top-down hypothesis. The bottom-up hypothesis, pioneered by Ulrich, says that forest soils are the key to the story.[1] A century of acid fallout from factory chimneys has made German soils acid. The acid has washed chemicals, which are important food for trees, out of the soil. And it has turned aluminium, a metal commonly and harmlessly found in soils, into a toxic form that can invade the cells of tree roots. 'Only when all this has happened and the roots are critically damaged does the rest of the tree suffer,' says Ulrich. Roots lose the ability to take up the nutrient chemicals, such as magnesium and calcium, from the soil. Yellow, magnesium-deficient needles are bad at photosynthesis – a process that creates sugars and starch by converting carbon dioxide from the air in sunlight. The tree starves to death.

The top-down hypothesis says that the decline starts with the needles. Air pollution attacks the needles, washing out magnesium. The roots try to make good the loss, but it becomes increasingly difficult and eventually the whole tree goes into decline. The main version of the top-down hypothesis claims that ozone damages the needles and acid rain and mists wash out the nutrients.[2]

Ulrich was the man who predicted the crisis. Yet as it unfolded through 1983 and 1984, his ideas fell out of fashion. Then in 1986 he was suddenly back in favour again among his German colleagues. So, was the man from the Solling forest right all along? There is plenty of evidence that German forest soils have become more acid in recent decades, and that acid in soils does wash away nutrients, including magnesium. Ulrich can also show that roots always seem to be damaged before the more visible parts of the tree show symptoms of decline. They become less dense and retract into the surface layers of the soil – for Norway spruce that can mean the top ten or twenty centimetres.

Ulrich's story sounds convincing and fits the known facts about what happens to soils and trees in an acid environment. But from the day he first expounded it, there have been doubts. Why did the trees of the dreadfully polluted Ruhr region not turn yellow and die decades ago? Why is damage worse in the mountains of southern Germany, where the air is apparently clearer and soils are often rich in lime, which neutralizes acid?[3] A stark image in the Black Forest is of masses of lichens, which are very sensitive to sulphur dioxide, growing on dying trees.

To answer these questions, scientists from Essen, in the heart of the Ruhr, and Munich, in the foothills of the Bavarian Alps, developed their top-down hypothesis. They say the key to the carnage is ozone, generated by Germany's 25 million cars. Bernhard Prinz from Essen is known as the 'prince of ozone'. He says that the concentrations of ozone that accumulate in the hills of Bavaria and the Black Forest damage the skin of needles and upset photosynthesis. The acid mists that also collect on the mountainsides invade the damaged needles and wash out nutrients. The mechanisms have been demonstrated in the lab. But Prinz's claim that the process cripples the tree is not demonstrated. Some scientists ask why, if the nutrients are washed from the needles into the soils, the roots find it so difficult to recover them again.

The chief attraction of Prinz's top-down hypothesis is that it explains the geography of *Waldsterben* best. Ozone, like *Waldsterben*, is found all over West Germany but is at its worst in the mountains of the south. Ozone, like *Waldsterben*, is a phenomenon of the last decade or so.

I turned to the Bavarians for a measured view. I went to Otto Lange at Wurzburg. He is an honest man, given to avoiding fashionable trends. He wears a white laboratory coat more often than a conference suit, dons a black French beret and drives a fifteen-year-old Mercedes. On his bookshelf I found, among yards of heavier tomes, a copy of John Wyndham's science fiction story, *Trouble With Lichen*. He told me:

We all look for effects in areas we know about. I am a botanist and I trust plants, but not the soil. I looked at first for direct effects on the plants from the air. Prinz's views were attractive. But our experiments here lead us to think otherwise. There is no doubt that in the lab you can show that ozone and acid mist do wash nutrients out of needles. But we see little evidence that this is happening to an important extent in the Bavarian forests.

The key test, for Lange, was to look for signs of worsening damage to needles that had been exposed for several years to ozone and acid. He reasoned that if the important damage is done directly to needles, then the rate of photosynthesis in needles on a tree should be related to the age of the needle But his experiments, clamping all manner of electronic equipment on to branches high up in the Fichtelgebirge mountains, revealed no such trend. The only distinction was between damaged needles that had lived through the hot dry summer of 1983 and those needles that had developed since. 'The evidence,' says Lange, 'strongly suggests that only a dry summer, when the soils become more acid and nutrients become more scarce, produces forest decline.'

It was this kind of evidence that led plant pathologists to criticize the top-downers at a conference of Germany's top experts on *Waldsterben* at the end of 1985. The evidence points to an effect derived from soils and triggered by the weather. It means Ulrich, rather than Prinz; bottom-up rather than top-down. Ozone or acid mists might help the process along. But the findings of the Bavarian scientists suggest that the answer does lie in the soil.

So far, we have two unsatisfactory explanations provided by two warring camps. Ulrich provides the more convincing mechanisms. Prinz's ideas fit the pattern of decline. Some key factor must be missing. There have been plenty of candidates. One week it is detergents, the next, lead in petrol. So at first nobody paid much attention when Dutch scientists claimed in 1982 that slurry from pig farms could be the magic ingredient.

Holland has a lot of pigs locked up in factory farms. It probably has a greater density of the beasts than anywhere else on earth. They all produce manure that is stored in slurry tanks and sprayed on to farmland as a fertilizer – or just to get rid of it. The manure contains lots of ammonia, some of which gets into the air. Manure in parts of the Netherlands emits more than 100 kilograms of ammonia per hectare per year. The national total is more than 100,000 tonnes a year. The ammonia mixes with sulphur dioxide, often ion foliage, to form ammonium sulphate.

The ammonia is greatly speeding up the transformation of sulphure dioxide to sulphate. In the soil, ammonium sulphate converts to both sulphuric and nitric acid. The Dutch scientists, headed by Dr N. van Breemen of the Agricultural University at Wageningen, found that up to three-quarters of the acid reaching soils in the Rouwkuilen nature reserve in Linburg came from ammonium sulphate.[4] The reserve is surrounded by factory farms.

Since the Dutch discovery, the idea of ammonia as a key to acidity has, as the cynics in the Russian jeep put it, 'spread like wildfire across Europe. It was all conjecture but everybody wanted to believe it.' The ammonium hypothesis was developed by Dutch, Swedish and German scientists. They say that ammonium fallout is adding so much nitrogen to the soil that forests everywhere are becoming 'saturated' with the stuff – gorged on one of their most important foods.[5]

It dawned on scientists that they had become so preoccupied with nitrogen as a source of nitric acid and ozone that they had forgotten how important it was to trees on its own. Somebody did some sums to show that up to fifty kilograms of nitrogen fall on a typical hectare of German forest each year. It comes both from car exhausts and from agricultural ammonia. Then it emerged that some foresters who today bemoan the loss of their trees had, until recently, boasted of record growth. Ulrich says: 'We still have forests that have never grown as well as now.' And he remembers how trees in the Harz mountains had obscured a hotel viewing platform shortly before they keeled over.

Trees cannot resist the temptations to eat nitrogen. 'No tree anywhere in the world does anything when given more nitrogen other than grow bigger,' says Schulze. The dying trees of Germany are never short of nitrogen. What they do not get through their roots, they pick up through their needles directly from polluted air.

But this apparent surviving strength may be fatal. The metabolism of a tree forces it to use all the nitrogen it has to keep on growing taller. This, says Schulze, 'only makes the shortage of other nutrients more critical'. It is rather like a starving human being force-fed sugar. A tree that should be husbanding its resources through hard times is forced instead to grow. Is this the missing factor?

The truth is that no German theory appears able to encompass, let alone explain, what is going on. No German scientist has been able to gather all the strands together. I finally found somebody who could in, of all places, Norway. Gunnar Abrahamsen runs the Norwegian Forest Research

Institute at As, a quiet dormitory town near Oslo. Apart perhaps from Ulrich, his pedigree in acid rain and forest decline goes back further than anybody's. He first started feeding artificial acid rain to trees back in 1972. Years before Ulrich went public, Abrahamsen had shown that acid washed nutrients from soils and stunted the growth of trees.[6] 'We were the first people to talk about magnesium deficiency as the root of decline,' he says. 'I thought when we finished our study in 1978 we had most of the answers. I still think that.' The Norwegian government has just got excited about the state of Norway's trees and is showering Abrahamsen with millions of kroner to resume his experiments. Wearily, he accepts the cash. 'German dieback has meant that we have had to continue our work. The political pressure is so great,' he says.

Abrahamsen has watched the frantic scientific scrambling in Germany with a studied detachment. When Ulrich first produced his apocalyptic vision of a treeless Germany, Abrahamsen was ready with his long-prepared analysis of 'the three main effects of acid rain on soils'. He presented them to a conference in London in 1983.[7] The first effect of acid rain is a fertilizing one, caused mostly by the deposition of nitrogen. The second is an acidification of soils. It happens because nutrients are washed out of the soil by the sulphate in acid rain, leaving behind the acid hydrogen ions. The third is the toxic effect on trees of aluminium liberated in those acid soils.

Abrahamsen's overview of how acid rain affects soils and waters goes like this. Much of the acid in soils today arises from the natural processes by which soils were formed on the bare rock left behind by the last ice age. Nevertheless, there is ample evidence from most of northern Europe that soils have become significantly more acid this century. In West Germany and Sweden, there has been a widespread decrease in pH by around one unit, equivalent to a tenfold increase in acidity.

Acid rain is almost certain to have caused the sudden change, he says. The driving force of this acidification is not the acid but, as we have seen, the sulphate that falls with it.

In most European soils of all types, sulphate is the agent that drags with it whatever will most readily combine with it. In the rich soils of central Europe the sulphate takes nutrient chemicals such as calcium and magnesium. In poor soils, as in most of Scandinavia, there are not many nutrients present. So the sulphate drags out hydrogen ions (that is, acid) and aluminium. This means that in most of central Europe soils become acid because the acid from the rain is left behind, while in Scandinavia, much of the acid departs with the sulphate and turns up in the rivers and lakes.

Nitrate and ammonia may today be responsible for half the acid in acid rain, but it is usually much less important than sulphate in turning soils and rivers acid. Except in winter, the nitrate is readily taken up by plants and little is left for other work. Recently however, soil scientists have found nitrate being washed out of forest soils in some places, usually in heavily polluted areas.

In the most polluted parts of northern Czechoslovakia, scientists found that 92 per cent of the nitrates entering forest soils came out again and went into rivers.[8] In the Solling forest, Ulrich's colleagues found that 60 per cent washed out. One study has found nitrates starting to leach from forest soils in the Black Forest, too. Such evidence is a clear sign that those soils have become saturated with nitrogen, says Abrahamsen. This could mean an effective doubling of the potential of the pollution to acidify soils and rivers. The nitrate ceases to have a fertilizing effect and switches to acidification.

Good soils, which carry plenty of nitrogen, may become saturated more quickly than poor ones, which start with a severe nitrogen deficiency, says Abrahamsen. Swedish scientists calculate that at levels of nitrogen fallout found today throughout Germany and central Europe, poor soils beneath spruce forests would become saturated with nitrogen in sixty-five years.[9] Better soils would take only twenty-five years. Given the history of pollution in Germany, the Swedes say this implies a crisis today on both types of soil there. This is because in West Germany, poor soils are found closer to the big centres of pollution in northern Germany, whereas better soils are found in 'cleaner' areas to the south of the country.

Put this way, we begin to have an explanation for the central problems of Ulrich's case. Trees are dying at least as much in the clean areas with good soils as in the dirty areas with poor soils because nitrogen saturation happens most quickly on the 'good' soils. And trees are suffering now because nitrate fallout in most of Europe has doubled in the past thirty years, bringing an entirely new dimension to the acid loading of soils.

None of this destroys other hypotheses about *Waldsterben*. Even Ulrich agrees that ozone may do some damage to trees 'in the final stages', when they can no longer get nutrients from the soil. But the nitrogen factor does underline the enormous potential of modern pollution to turn soils acid – and the role of car exhausts in that process.

What can be done? Ulrich believes that some soils are so destroyed by acid that trees have become dependent for nutrients on what falls from the skies. 'They live in a solution culture,' he says. 'In some places the first effect of cutting pollution may be to starve trees of essential nutrients.' Nevertheless, reducing pollution is the only way forward. But Ulrich warns: 'Cutting emissions and allowing natural regeneration would take decades or centuries. The lost minerals can eventually be replaced by the slow, natural weathering of rocks beneath the soil, and these chemicals will in turn slowly neutralize the acid.'

Anything faster will require the massive application of lime, magnesium and fertilizers on to forest soils. It might cost £15 billion, says Ulrich. But nobody knows the true cost – or whether it would work at all.

The Alps Laid Bare

The people of Bristen, high in the Swiss Alps, are used to evacuating parts of their town when winter avalanches threaten. But now, they say, the 'safe houses' are becoming unsafe. They fear that the giant Bristenstock mountain, which towers over their valley, could unleash an avalanche that would cover the whole of Bristen. The problem is that the beech, fir and pine trees on the slopes above the town have become infested with bark beetle.[10] The infestation, which is widespread in Switzerland today, is often connected with air pollution. One theory is that the changes in amino acids noted in trees under assault from air pollution make the tree more attractive to the beetle.

The canton's foresters have cut down the infested trees to prevent the spread of the beetle. But in the Alps trees are the main defence against avalanches. They both hold back an avalanche hurtling down the hillside, and break the fall of new snow, which is often the trigger for avalanches. Denuded mountainsides are not just an eyesore, they are potentially deadly. In the summer of 1985, Bristeners built huge soil terraces above the town, where they plan to plant new trees. The mayor of Bristen, Hans Murer, said he wanted three million francs for a concrete barrier to keep out avalanches. And in the winter of 1985–6 parts of Bristen were evacuated for fear that the denuded slopes would trigger a disaster.

There is something drastically wrong with the trees of the Alps. *Waldsterben* appears to have spread from the German Alps to Switzerland, Austria and France. Even the Alpine fastness of Lichtenstein reports damage. In an area of Europe stretching from central France to Poland there are 60,000 square kilometres of damaged forests – perhaps a sixth of which are in serious decline. Sometimes, the trees lose their needles or become yellow and thin; sometimes, as in Bristen, they become infected with disease.

The Swiss forestry office reported at the end of 1986 that almost a half of Swiss trees were sick. In the mountain canton of Uri, where Bristen is situated, 90 per cent of the white fir and 50 per cent of the red fir and pine are ill.

Much of the disease is minor. But the Swiss environment minister Alphons Egli says: 'The situation in the mountain forests is dramatic.' The forestry office warns that a tenth of the 'barrier forests' that protect against avalanches in the Alps are likely to be lost in the next few years. This would put 150,000 people at risk and, if the skiing tourists who flock to the area each year get to hear of it, could undermine the area's biggest industry.

They tell the same story in the Bavarian Alps. A local paper there warns that 'Europe's winter playground could become a depopulated and treeless wilderness of barren rock and scree within fifteen years.' This may sound alarmist, but almost 80 per cent of the trees in parts of the German Alps are classified as sick.[11] The area is noted for its fir trees, which are only rarely found elsewhere in Germany. Damage to firs was first noted there in the 1970s. Today 87 per cent of German fir trees are classified as damaged. More than two-thirds are placed by foresters in the most severe categories, where disease is unambiguous. The proportion of fir trees in these categories is almost three times the proportion of Norway spruce which, because of its predominance across the rest of Germany, has received most attention. Successive surveys show *Waldsterben* spreading faster among firs than among other species.

The German forest survey for 1985 said the state of firs was

very alarming ... In the Alps they are of great silvicultural and ecological importance ... The strong transition from slight damage to severe damage ... continues to occur with the same intensity. The very existence of this valuable tree species must be regarded as being acutely at stake.

Across the border, around Salzburg in Austria, the fir forests in this holiday area show similar symptoms. And a survey conducted by the French National Forestry Office during 1985 also found damage to trees most severe among the firs of the French Alps. More than a quarter had lost at least 25 per cent of their needles. The proportion of fir trees damaged reached 40 per cent in the Chartreuse area, close to the Italian border.

The fir tree is a sensitive tree. It has suffered periodic setbacks over the past two centuries. But there seems little doubt that the present catastrophe is more severe, more widespread and more persistent than past bouts. But even though the decline has been evident for a decade there are remarkably few clues as to what is causing it. There are no general signs of attack from virus, bug or fungus. Until recently it was assumed that Alpine air was clean. Now we know that high concentrations of ozone build up there, especially in southern Germany and Switzerland. But what evidence there is suggests that fir trees are unusually tolerant of ozone, at any rate in the lab. It may be acid rain or acid mists or acid in the soil. It may have the same cause as the epidemic of yellow needles among Norway spruce in Germany – or it may not. Until somebody investigates, we will not know.

The Dutch state forestry commission has done better in investigating its version of *Waldsterben*. Its study in 1985 found that 13 per cent of Dutch forests suffered from serious disease. 'A large part of these forests are probably not able to restore themselves if the conditions causing their health problem do not change.' The commission looked at soils and found that 'damage to health is most clear on soils sensitive to acidification.' It found that neither exposure to wind nor shortage of water in the soil seemed to be important factors for the general decline. It discovered that a fungus called Diplodia pinea 'is spread all through the Netherlands and concentrates in the forest areas with the worst health'. That might mean that the fungus is responsible for the decline, or that it is rather good at invading sick forests in acid soils. The Dutch foresters have concluded that the latter is most likely. Many scientists have noticed that fungi thrive best in acid soils. The Dutch say that 'the severe damage occurs when the nitrogen concentration in the needles is higher than normal.' They believe that the most likely source of this damaging nitrogen is fallout of ammonium sulphate created by pollution from the country's factory farms. They conclude that 'the influence of air pollution is the most important factor defining the health of Dutch forests.'

A Very British Malaise

In the summer of 1984, Joachim Puhe, a German forester, spent five days touring Britain looking for sick trees. He came at the invitation of Friends of the Earth in Scotland. Seeing the huge political controversy stirred up in West Germany by the Green Party over sick trees, Friends of the

Earth wanted a slice of the action. When Puhe, a colleague of Bernhardt Ulrich's at the University of Gottingen, reached the Lake District, he could not believe his luck. He discovered huge areas of trees with browned needles and lost shoots. 'If we had observed these signs in Germany we would have classified them as being caused by acid rain,' Puhe reported.

It did not take Friends of the Earth long to point out that the rain-swept hills of the Lake District have more acid fallout than almost anywhere in Britain. It did not take long for the Forestry Commission, which runs most of Britain's large upland plantations of conifer trees, to realize that it had some explaining to do. Did it stand by its claim that there was no evidence of damage from acid rain in Britain? Or did it sign up with the greens?

The commission was most embarrassed that it had taken a foreign forester on a five-day whistle-stop tour to spot what it now admits was a major, unexplained epidemic. 'We are concerned that local staff had not reported it earlier,' says John Gibbs at the commission's research headquarters outside Farnham in Surrey. 'These days they spend all day logging stock yields on their computers, rather than being out in the forests,' he told me. In 1985, the commission inaugurated a 'damage-monitoring day' on which staff will file away their computer print-outs, put on their gumboots and go out looking for sick trees.

The epidemic covered a wide area of northern England and Scotland, from the Lake District to Sutherland – a distance of 400 kilometres. And there were reports of similar damage to fir trees in central Wales, with brown needles in Haffren forest, for instance. Echoing the German experience, the damage was worst at higher altitudes and among older trees. And it affected different species, apparently indiscriminately. A report on the affair from the commission's scientists said: 'Severe foliage browning and shoot death was observed on Sitka spruce, Norway spruce, Scots pine, Lodgepole pine, Douglas fir and Grand fir . . . Detailed examination showed an essentially similar pattern of symptoms on all species.'[12] Several years' shoots often died 'resulting in the death of substantial second order branches.' In all cases, damage occurred in the top half of the tree's crown, but avoiding the topmost branches.

Derek Redfern, a scientist from the commission's research station near Edinburgh, claims to have seen signs of damage from his office window in March 1984. Large organizations being what they are, there was no follow-up, even though the same symptoms were eventually found among trees covering several thousand hectares. Redfern admits: 'The damage bears striking similarities to damage that occurs in Germany.' Nothing like it had been seen by the commission's scientists in Britain before.[13]

Confusion was compounded when the damage appeared to go away again as fast as it arrived. Gibbs says: 'The browning was gone by August. The trees look as good as new now.' With sighs of relief all round, Gibbs and his colleagues concluded that air pollution had not been involved in the incident.

The public version today is that high winds and sudden changes in temperature that winter were to blame for the damage. 'Top-dying' and the browning of needles due to windy winters is a well-known problem for Norway spruce which 'greatly restricts its use', the commission says. But the scientists remain concerned. The following year, they wrote: 'since the precise mechanism of damage remains unknown the possibility has to be considered that trees were pre-disposed to climatic injury by other environmental factors.'[12] This is a euphemism, of course. As one of the commission's best scientists, David Lonsdale, put it to me: 'It is not our role to complain about pollution *per se*, however much we do not like it.'

There is disturbing evidence that something odd has been happening to the trees of Cumbria for some years. During cross-questioning at a conference late in 1984, Redfern revealed that some of the young trees there have almost stopped growing. 'In most individuals there was a growth reduction,' he said, 'down to as much as a quarter of the growth rate in the early 1970s.'[13] In some cases the decline began a decade ago; in others only in the 1980s. Everybody is now waiting to see if the symptoms recur. Meanwhile, the commission has begun its own limited national tree survey, along the lines of the Germany surveys.

For Chris Rose, a lanky, fast-thinking, slow-talking, acid-rain campaigner at Friends of the Earth, the events of 1984 were a godsend. Here, perhaps, was the key to unlocking the environmental conscience of the British in the cause of acid rain. His big problem was that the British do not like the conifer plantations inflicted in the past sixty years on the once-bare uplands of their country. Many would be happy if acid rain destroyed the lot. So Rose set out to find evidence that trees in the countryside of England were damaged, too. In 1985 he enlisted 500 volunteers to investigate two species: the beech and the yew. The volunteers were sent off to look for a list of symptoms including leaf curl, green leaf fall and 'cluster twigs'. The results were startling. Sixty-nine per cent of beech trees and 78 per cent of yews were recorded as showing signs of damage.[14] Rose admits that his observers would be almost bound to head for damaged tree stands. 'The evidence is circumstantial, we admit it, but there is a lot of it,' he said, when launching the results of the survey.

'There are enormous numbers of dying yew trees in the Lake District. Their needles should last six or eight years. But this year they were yellowing and dying at two or three years old.' He claimed to have jumbled up slides from London Richmond Park and West Germany. 'You can't tell the difference.' Beech trees on sandy soils, from the New Forest in Hampshire to the Sussex Weald were 'severely damaged'. A designated site of special scientific interest at Wyndcliffe in the Wye valley was devastated. 'The Henley area has stands of beech indistinguishable from those at lower elevations in the Black Forest.'

There were gaffes, of course. It turns out that Bagley Wood in Oxfordshire showed 'extensive dieback' because a new bypass had blocked off the wood's drainage and the trees had become waterlogged. But support for his overall claims was extensive. The staff of the Snowdonia National Park sent in a return for the study. A note appended to it said: 'We see little point in completing the beech survey since so many beeches in north Wales are showing the exact symptoms you mention.' Rod Gritten, who completed the form, told me that sycamore, the traditional windbreak round farms in the area, had suffered recently, along with yew, lime and hornbeam. 'Nobody really notices the trends. Local farmers have poor memories for the details of trees. But foresters here agree that this year is particularly bad.'

Against Rose's anecdotal, circumstantial data, there is the Forestry Commission's own survey of trees. It is scientific, but its conclusion, that there is little cause for alarm, has little more credibility than Rose's data.[15] The commission looked only at commercial plantations, and at young trees (which in Germany were seen to suffer much less damage). It omitted trees on the edge of stands, because they might suffer other stresses such as wind damage. As angry exchanges over the two surveys reached a peak in November 1985, Rose was able to score heavily. 'Damage is known to be worst in older trees, on wind-blown escarpments and on the edge of plantations. Young trees inside plantations are not damaged. Yet these are what the Forestry Commission decided to look at,' he said. 'It is elsewhere, in the gardens, churchyards and hedgerows, among the great majority of the nation's trees, that damage is found.'[16] And with that Rose flew to Geneva for a new job with the World Wildlife Fund where his campaigning skills command a salary three times what Friends of the Earth paid him.

In his brief foray into tree pathology, Rose had generated a lot of heat. Traditional practitioners were angry with what they regarded as his betrayal of scientific principles. But he had also dragged into the open what many scientists in other disciplines regard as slackness and lack of rigour among the tree people. Too many assumptions and not enough experiments. It is the same problem that has bedevilled the Germans in their attempts to get to grips with what is happening to their trees. The only difference, as Rose points out, is that 'while much of the German damage is attributed to pollution, all of the British damage is put down to weather, aphids or fungi'.

There are two problems. What level of sickness in a

community of trees can you regard as 'natural'? And, in such complex and long-lasting organisms, how do you decide what is wrong when they do become sick? In its own survey, the Forestry Commission found that a third of Sitka spruce had 10 per cent of their needles missing, but only one in twenty had more than 25 per cent missing. The commission's scientists say that any loss less than 25 per cent is normal. For Rose the findings 'look much like the Germany survey of 1983'. The commission found that more than half the Scots pines it looked at were damaged. It blames this on insects, fungi and winds. But it is not so long ago that the commission gave exactly these reasons to explain why the same trees would not grow on the southern Pennines. Now it accepts that pollution was to blame there.

The argument in Britain over what makes a tree sick has been fought principally over the beech tree – a much-loved regular of the English countryside. Rose brought a second foreign scientist, a Swedish plant ecologist called Bent Nilghard, to Britain in 1985. Nilghard reported: 'In a journey between London and Bristol I did not find a single healthy beech tree.' Shoots that began life twelve to fifteen years ago were only a few centimetres long, where they should have been a metre or more long. Leaves were going yellow and dropping off during the second week of August. 'These are exactly the same symptoms as in central Europe,' he said. Nilghard later wrote to the Forestry Commission, which had complained about his well-publicized trip through its fiefdom. 'I must repeat that what I saw in England really made me nervous; your trees showed allover so much symptoms [sic].'

David Lonsdale at the commission is an acknowledged expert on the beech tree. He agreed in 1966 that the beech has problems. 'Certainly, as you drive around, hedgerow trees look very thin. A lot of beech trees are not well this year.' Why? 'The drought of 1975 and 1976 hit many trees very hard, especially old trees,' he says. 'Then the droughts of 1983 and 1984 produced bad growth in 1985. The drought was worst in the west and Wales – that explains the problems with beech trees in Snowdonia, for example.' While younger trees may recover from drought, older ones may go into permanent decline, he says.

Days before Friends of the Earth began their survey of beech trees, Lonsdale was told, 'from on very high' as he put it, to conduct his own. Lonsdale says that more than 80 per cent of the trees he looked at were healthy. But, once again, there were problems in the Lake District. 'I saw early yellowing of leaves everywhere there from the third week of August,' he told me. 'It was alarming. The cool, dull summer following a drought was perhaps enough to do it. But if it occurs again I would be worrying.'

There are clearly problems in explaining why hot, dry summers sometimes damage beech trees, and on other occasions, cool, dull summers do the same. But there is a more serious and general issue. The commission says its scientists always seek to explain damage to trees in terms of known agents – fungi, drought or whatever. These are the things they know about. But if, as many people believe, pollution is to be seen as another stress factor working in combination with these 'natural' stresses, then this approach will miss new stresses unless they produce new and unambiguous symptoms. The effects of air pollutants must be looked for specifically in the forests and hedgerows. It is not enough to be able to 'explain' everything in other terms.

From Geneva, Rose's view remains the same. 'The commission has failed to explain the widespread occurrence of symptoms that are strikingly similar to those attributed to acid rain on the continent.' He has won some interesting and powerful friends. William Waldegrave told MPs late in 1985 that the commission's own surveys were not good enough and he wanted the Institute of Terrestrial Ecology, the government's own research organization, to conduct a survey of the state of the nation's trees. He warned specifically that 'multi-stress analysis' would be needed.

The last word, perhaps, should come from Professor Fred Last, a deputy director of the institute. 'I don't agree with some of Friends of the Earth's conclusions. But many trees today have characteristics that are not healthy. Rose is entitled to expect more rigorous answers than he has been given.'

Last is proud of his expertise in the field of plant health and he has massive amounts of data at his fingertips in his office at Penicuik, outside Edinburgh. He warns that it is dangerous to be too precious about the scientific quality of such information. 'Our data bank on the distribution of plants in the UK is almost all derived from work by interested outsiders,' he says. 'There is a feeling here and at the Department of the Environment that we would like to use the expertise and enthusiasm of Friends of the Earth's investigators – perhaps having them join Forestry Commission people in classes in how to spot damage. We have to learn how to use these people,' he says.

If British scientists are confused about what is happening in the forests, they have shown much greater energy in analysing the impact of air pollutants on crops. A large part of the international literature on the sensitivity of plants to sulphur dioxide, and now nitrogen oxides and ozone, comes from British universities, such as Nottingham, Lancaster and Imperial College, London.

Unfortunately, as Fred Last says, 'little of the voluminous literature is of immediate relevance. Mostly it overlooks the fact that pollutants occur in mixtures.'[17] It turns out that sulphur dioxide is much more dangerous when mixed with nitrogen dioxide or with ozone – something which happens in the real world all the time, but which nobody looked at in the lab until recently.

Still, a new start is being made. One of the leading exponents is Mike Ashmore, who tends his plants from a converted insect house at a research station run by Imperial College outside Ascot, in the stockbroker belt west of London. Ashmore and his colleagues have been keeping plants in open-top chambers since 1976. These chambers (actually ramshackle plastic contraptions with a habit of blowing down in winter) allow experimenters to pump in heavy doses of particular chemicals, while keeping the plants exposed to the open air and its attendant pollutants. That way you pick up the all important effects of combinations of pollutants.

Many important crops are sensitive to ozone and other gaseous pollutants at the levels typically found in Britain. But acid soils rarely trouble them because so much lime is routinely put on farmland that soils are unlikely to go acid. (The comparison with trees is interesting. Trees are less sensitive in the lab to ozone. But they live in soil that is not routinely limed and so is at much greater risk of acidification.)

Barley can produce smaller harvests either after exposure to sulphur dioxide in winter or from ozone in summer. Legumes – peas, beans and the like – are most susceptible to ozone attack. Since 1976, Ashmore has found four occasions when leaves on spinach or radishes have been killed by ozone.[18] They were the beginning of June 1978, early August 1981, mid-July 1983, and during 1984. Spinach, radishes and barley have all been shown by Ashmore's people to have been damaged by ozone in the past ten years.

During the hot summers of 1983 and 1984, Ashmore put four varieties of pea plants into bags with a standard soil and left them to grow at eighteen sites along the forty kilometres between Ascot and central London. At each site, pollution was measured. Rabbits, caterpillars and even hungry humans ate many of the plants. Among those that survived there was a remarkable gradation in the size of the pea crop. For each of the pea varieties, the crop was about half as large in central London as in Ascot.[19] Ozone levels did not differ much between London and Ascot, but other pollutants did. Ashmore believes that 'it is the enhanced effect of ozone together with sulphur dioxide and nitrogen dioxide which is responsible for the reduction in pea yields'.

In another study made during a dull, low-ozone summer in 1977, Ashmore found that a tobacco plant, which is especially sensitive to ozone, was damaged to varying degrees by the gas over most of Britain.[20] He concluded: 'Ozone concentrations sufficient to damage our test plants can occur anywhere in the British Isles, with the possible exception of northern Scotland.'

Levels of ozone in Britain often reach fifty parts per billion in apparently clean air, and rise to three or four times that figure during ozone smogs. For a sensitive, but commercially important plant such as the pea, Ashmore believes that if ozone levels get much above fifty parts per billion for more than seven hours a day for ten days running, this will produce a visible effect on the plant. And for key crops such as barley he says: 'My feeling is that if more than 10 per cent of days get above sixty parts per billion of ozone then you may start to see declines in crops.' There is likely to be a drop in yield from such crops long before any visible sign of injury appears on foliage. His findings are backed up by research in the USA which finds drops in yield of crops such as tomatoes and soybeans whenever average daytime levels of ozone rise above forty parts per billion during the growing season. One estimate puts the value of this lost crop at $2 billion a year.

Ashmore is an avowed 'ozone man'. He believes that the exceptionally wide distribution of ozone in rural areas makes it especially dangerous for crops. Other people, such as Professor Terry Mansfield at Lancaster University, believe that sulphur dioxide and nitrogen dioxide are more important. What seems to matter most is that each of these pollutants is much more lethal in combination with the others than separately. Mansfield suggests that nitrogen dioxide may be a key. It is highly toxic, but is normally broken down quickly and apparently harmlessly by leaves. This process is disrupted by sulphur dioxide, however. Separately, the two gases are pretty harmless, except at concentrations rarely seen today. Together they are dangerous.[21]

Sometimes the effects can be even more unexpected. Some of Ashmore's colleagues have shown that in south-east England the widespread black-bean aphid shows 'consistently higher concentrations ... in an area downwind of London and in the proximity of heavy industry'.[22] It is not that the aphid likes pollution, rather that the pollution changes the balance of amino acids in the bean plant in such a way that the bug can dine off it better. Peter Dohmen, who co-wrote this important study, is now in West Germany. There he reports that aphids grow 20 per cent better on rose bushes in

Munich air than in clean air. Such findings, he says, 'indicate a strong possibility that air pollution has a serious economic impact on crop productivity as a result of increased pest incidence'.[23] Sure enough, it turns out that there was a massive infestation of aphids running rampant through the cereal crops of southern England during the long, hot summer of 1976, when ozone levels reached new (and still unsurpassed) highs. They were 'feasting on the juices of plants and spreading virus diseases to healthy crops', according to *The Times*.[24]

In the summer of 1911, scientists in Leeds found that lettuces in Garforth, a village eleven kilometres east of the city, grew three to four times as large as those grown in the same soil in the centre of Leeds.[19] Then, smoke and sulphur dioxide were to blame. Those pollutants are now declining. The new pollutants are nitrogen dioxide and ozone caused by the new scourge, the car. Whatever the detail of the processes involved, it is clear that farmers have no cause to be sanguine because smoke is almost gone and sulphur dioxide is abating. Ashmore's pea study, with its striking resemblance to the lettuce study of seventy years before, is clear enough evidence of that.

5   In The Clouds

Ozone: The New Menace

Saturday 3 July 1976 was the hottest day of one of the hottest, sunniest, driest summers ever in south-east England. The weather was big news. Papers were already reporting 'the worst drought for 250 years' and that day *The Times* led with the news: 'Water shortage to be tackled by emergency powers bill.' Blooms had wilted at the centenary show of the Royal National Rose Society (the Queen Mother in attendance). In Wiltshire, the harvest was already under way, just in time to beat an infestation of aphids. Troops were fighting heath fires from Surrey to Dorset, and in Invernesshire a forest fire was advancing along a six-kilometre front.

But the papers missed the big story. Ozone, the pollutant that had stalked Los Angeles since the 1940s but had barely been noticed in Europe, was blanketing western Europe from Scotland to northern Italy. Concentrations were far greater than ever recorded before on the continent.

Ozone is generated in the soup of modern air pollutants, especially when it is hot, sunny and dry. It is difficult to disentangle the effects of ozone from those of heat, sun and drought. But what most people call a summer heat haze is in fact a haze of pollutants, most of them acid, created by ozone. Some scientists wonder whether ozone was responsible for some of the extra deaths that occurred in south-east England during the hottest part of the summer of 1976. And some believe that ozone, as much as the drought, was responsible for the serious sickness that afflicted many beech trees in Britain the following year.

Levels of ozone in Europe today are already routinely high enough to damage sensitive crops and humans. On a cloudy day when little new ozone is being created in the air, average levels are between ten and fifty parts per billion (ppb). This is probably due about equally to incursions of ozone from the upper stratosphere and to pollution from man. In south-east England in the long, hot summer of 1976, as the chemistry of ozone generation went into overdrive, concentrations soared above 200 ppb and hit 260 ppb on Saturday 3 July. Damage to sensitive plants begins, as we have seen, at 50 ppb.

The amount of ozone considered safe for a factory worker to breathe in during a working day is 80 ppb. The figure was 'exceeded at all our sites in the outside air in south-east England for the equivalent of a working week', according to government air chemists in their report on the event.[1]

'LA', as the song has it, 'is a great big freeway'. There are almost as many cars there as people. Ozone is created in greatest quantities by cars, so it is no surprise that ozone smogs were found first in Los Angeles. But the number of cars in western Europe has soared in the past thirty years. In Switzerland and southern Germany, there is more than one car for every two and a half people. So now Europe has an ozone problem, too.

Along with carbon monoxide and lead, the main pollutants from car exhausts are nitrogen oxides and various hydrocarbons. In sunlight, these react together to create a mass of different chemicals known as photo-oxidants. Much the most dangerous of them is ozone. The formation of photo-oxidants takes time to build up, peaking after perhaps five hours. So if there is any sort of summer breeze in the air, the gases given off by the millions of vehicles in a big city will generate most ozone in the countryside.

On our July Saturday, the highest levels of ozone were found not in London, but in Oxfordshire. Perversely, as Londoners drove out of the city to sample the delights of the English countryside in a glorious summer, their chemical soup followed them, to settle on their picnic sites that afternoon, causing coughs, stinging eyes and obscuring the views with haze.

Hot, sunny, ozone-breeding weather in Europe almost

always means the presence on weather charts of a large stationary zone of high pressure over the continent. Winds are light, and everybody hopes that the fat, slovenly anticyclone will stay put. In June and July 1976, one such high hung around for three scorching weeks. But if the high hangs around, so does the air in it. As the days pass, more and more ozone is generated and the air mass becomes more and more polluted. The air moves slowly across the continent, picking up a new load of pollution from each big city along the way. The ozone in the air decays only slowly. In Britain, the winds are usually from the east on these occasions. So rather than getting the usual clean, Atlantic air on which to export pollution, Britain is instead the last European port of call for the rest of the continent's pollution.

On our July Saturday, the air which brought record amounts of ozone to Oxfordshire picnickers had travelled across the Upper Silesian coalfield of southern Poland the previous Wednesday. By Friday afternoon, it was coasting in brilliant sunlight across the maze of autobahns in West Germany, and skirting the Ruhr before a night-flight across the English Channel. It acquired an extra early-morning dose of hydrocarbons from the oil refineries at Canvey Island in the Thames estuary, before gorging itself on the exhaust emissions of London.[1] South-west Ireland is the most western point in Europe. It is thousands of kilometres from the great industrial areas of the continent and is blasted almost daily by fresh, Atlantic air. It is everybody's idea of a clean environment. Until 1973, that included the air chemists. That year, they launched a study of ozone levels in Europe. 'The most remote site, at Adrigole in County Cork, was chosen in the expectation that it would provide a measure of the "background" level of ozone concentrations for the maritime regions of north-west Europe,' they said. What they found was rather different.

On three successive days that August, concentrations of ozone in the air of County Cork exceeded 100 ppb, way above the 'background' level.[2] The ozone seemed to have come from France, or perhaps farther east, on breezes generated by a high pressure area in the North Sea. But it had spent two days passing over the sea before arriving in County Cork. There can be little doubt that, when the conditions are right, a pall of ozone smog can cover most of Europe. It can expose hundreds of millions of people to concentrations of the gas that are known to be dangerous. Because of the complex chemistry involved, some of the highest concentrations can occur in some of the most unlikely places.

I have already mentioned that the time-lag involved in the formation of ozone means that the countryside is often worse hit by ozone than the cities. But there is a second reason for this. For, while nitrogen oxides coming from car exhausts are a prime cause of ozone formation, they can also destroy ozone. The process works like this. What emerges from car exhausts and power station chimneys is nitric oxide. This gas is converted in the air to nitrogen dioxide. It is nitrogen dioxide that reacts with the hydrocarbons – from car exhausts, chemical works, oil refineries and the like – to create ozone. But, while it survives, nitric oxide will break ozone back down again. Indeed, it is rather fast and efficient at it. So scientists often find a 'dip' in ozone levels in cities, towns and even beside motorways. Around London, polluted air moving in off the North Sea will have high levels of ozone as it passes over Suffolk and Essex, lower levels over London as ozone is destroyed, and then, as the pollutants from London begin to convert into ozone, higher amounts still as it reaches Hampshire or Oxfordshire. British monitoring points at Sibton in Suffolk and Harwell in Oxfordshire consistently have higher amounts of ozone than those in central London. The same phenomenon has been seen elsewhere in Europe. The highest ozone figures currently seen anywhere in Europe are created by the sunny, car-ridden metropolis of Athens. They can reach 350 ppb, and are found not in Athens itself, but in the countryside around.

Lord Marshall of Goring has the accent of a Welsh hill-farmer. He is a large, voluble man, given to glad-handing and being calculatedly indiscreet for journalists. He is also chairman of Britain's biggest polluter, the Central Electricity Generating Board. He was in confident mood on a cold winter day in December 1985, when he took a coachload of London journalists north to the giant Fiddlers Ferry power station on Merseyside. They were going to watch him turn on a new boiler, designed to halve the amount of nitrogen oxides expelled from the station's giant chimney.

Marshall was anxious to be seen responding quickly to the growing concern in Europe that ozone, caused in part by nitrogen oxides, was killing trees. With a price-tag of around a million pounds the equipment was less than a hundredth of the cost of equipment to cut emissions of sulphur. Marshall also revealed plans to spend another million pounds to measure the chemistry of ozone formation. Then, over lunch, he settled down to sow the seeds of doubt. 'It would,' he roared, 'make me laugh so much, I would laugh so much if it turned out that by cutting our nitrogen emissions we actually increased the production of ozone.'

He made the idea sound like a twinkle in his eye. He is after all, a former chief scientist at the Department of Energy. In fact, his own scientists had reported three months earlier their calculation that halving urban emissions of nitrogen oxides in London would increase ozone concentrations locally 'in one case by 27 per cent'. Nobody is about to contest the figure.[3] Even Norway's atmospheric chemists, who do not often see eye to eye with their counterparts at the generating board, agree. Unless emissions of hydrocarbons were reduced at the same time, a lowering of nitrogen-oxide levels would increase ozone formation in and around big cities such as London. In such places, nitric oxide devours more ozone than nitrogen dioxide can create.

This argument is great propaganda for the electricity board. But it is only a small corner of the ozone story. What happens away from the cities? By the time air reaches the countryside, the nitric oxide are is gone, converted to nitrogen dioxide. That is when the ozone generation gets going. And that is when the advantages of emitting less nitrogen oxides from cars and power stations shows up.

Unless it falls in acid rain, most of the nitrogen oxides in the atmosphere will eventually get converted to ozone or another photo-oxidant. The only question is where. If there are lots of reactive hydrocarbons from cars around, the transformation will, given a sunny day, happen sooner and so closer to the cities. If there are fewer hydrocarbons – after a crackdown on hydrocarbon pollution, perhaps – it will happen later.

One of Europe's top ozone chemists is a Norwegian who worked with British experts in the late 1970s. While in Britain, Oystein Hov of the University of Oslo worked on a successful computer model of ozone production in south-east England. It tried to account for the role of thirty-five different kinds of hydrocarbons and more than 300 chemical reactions.[4] It was published in 1979 and demonstrated more or less what Marshall was teasing journalists with six years later.

In cities, national controls on nitrogen oxides alone could do harm. In the surrounding countryside, such controls would cut ozone levels, though not by a great deal. Hov's British colleagues, such as Dick Derwent, say they now believe controls on hydrocarbons in car exhausts would be the most efficient method of cutting ozone levels in southern England on hot, sunny days. This, Hov says, is fine as far as it goes, which is roughly from Southampton to Ipswich. Not very useful if you live in Cork or Oslo or Corsica. And not, he suggests, if you plan to live on planet earth for much longer, either.

Hov's current concern is with what happens after the two or three days with which the British modellers were concerned. What happens in the big photochemical smogs which, as in 1976, can last for weeks on end? And what happens when the smog is dispersed and the pollution moves away from the ground and into the higher atmosphere, a kilometre or more above the ground? The answer is quite a lot.

Robert Guicherit, the Netherlands' top ozone specialist, puts it this way: 'The control of reactive hydrocarbons alone merely delays the production of ozone . . . Nitrogen dioxide will be transported out of the industrialized and urban areas into rural areas.'

One clue is the apparent sharp increase in the background concentrations of ozone in 'clean' air over Europe. Data from both East and West Germany show this background level has doubled in the past thirty years. This suggests that half of the current ozone background is man-made.

Hov says most of this ozone is being created slowly in the free troposphere. It forms from reactions between the unused nitrogen dioxide and a whole range of hydrocarbons, some barely considered before because they react slowly and have few short-term effects. 'Vehicle emissions, solvents and oil refineries are the sources of the more reactive hydrocarbons that have their big effect on the boundary layer,' says Hov. 'Many of the less reactive species, which create ozone in the free troposphere, come from the gas industry.' We are talking about a lot of gas here. Some 6 per cent of all the methane extracted from beneath the North Sea leaks away before it reaches the gas tap.

Methane takes years to react with nitrogen dioxide rather than the hours, or weeks, required by most of the other species. Methane comes from natural gas, farting animals, the belching of cows and other ruminants, from carcasses and from paddy fields. One recent estimate is that methane levels in the troposphere have risen by 30 per cent in the past thirty years. This methane may be very important in the chain of chemical reactions that are creating the ever-increasing background concentrations of ozone at ground level. But Hov believes that the factors that limit ozone creation in the troposphere are the amount of sunshine and the amount of nitrogen dioxide from power stations and cars. Lord Marshall should stop laughing at this point.

One calculation is that man's current activities on the farm and on the autobahn will lead to a further doubling of the ozone in the air in the next century.[5] If this happens, it will have a 'greenhouse effect', rather as carbon dioxide does, absorbing radiation from the sun and acting as a thermal blanket, warming the surface of the earth. It will also mean that all of Europe's plants become permanently exposed to concentrations of ozone that are known to cause damage. And it will mean that all of Europe's humans become almost permanently exposed to levels of ozone that are now considered unsafe for workers to be exposed to for a forty-hour week. Hov has a clear message: 'We have to stop arguing about city versus countryside. We must protect both. We must stop arguing between cutting nitrogen oxides or hydrocarbons. We have to cut both.'

Summer Smogs for the 1990s

The Eggborough power station in Yorkshire is the kind of giant electricity factory that the Norwegians believe is killing their fish. It is one of the 'unholy Trinity' – Drax, Ferry-bridge and Eggborough – on the Selby coalfield. Its gases form a plume, an expanding cone of pollution that leaves its 200-metre chimney and blows with the winds for hundreds of miles. The prevailing winds will take the plume north-east, past York, over the Yorkshire wolds and across the North Sea to Norway and the Arctic.

Tall chimneys save local farms and villages from a direct hit from power stations. The Eggborough plume usually takes about an hour before it touches the ground. But most of the pollution is blown on out to sea. The Norwegians say this means more of it falls on them. Bernie Fisher, the generating board's expert in this field, says that, on average, tall chimneys increase pollution over Norway by perhaps 20 per cent. 'Some people might say that is a lot,' he agrees. But the generating's board's official line is that such a figure is trivial. In any case, much depends on the weather.

The generating board's chemists have spent more than a million pounds 'tagging' the Eggborough plume with a harmless chemical and flying aircraft crammed full with monitoring equipment to find out where the plume goes and what happens to it. On one occasion, the flying chemists discovered the plume intact a day later and 650 kilometres away, just off the Danish coast.[6] Usually, however, the plume breaks up over the North Sea and mixes with the air of the 'boundary layer' – the bottom part of the atmosphere where weather happens. This sounds like a good thing. 'Dilute and disperse' is the catch-phrase that describes this very British approach to pollution control. But once the mixing begins, the increasingly reactive chemical soup that makes up the air over Europe today gets to work. It is this soup that is so efficient at turning sulphur dioxide and nitrogen oxides into sulphuric acid and nitric acid. And it is here that the links between acid and ozone formation appear.

The scientific purpose of the generating board's flying chemists has been to analyse the soup at work. The political purpose, some say, has been to confuse the issue, while looking for evidence that the other contents of the soup are so important in determining how much acid is formed that the exact content of the power station's plume itself does not matter much. The key question is: if the generating board cut its output of sulphur from power stations by, say, 30 per cent, would the amount of acid created over Norway and Scotland also fall by 30 per cent? Or would it just mean that a greater proportion of its sulphur would become converted to acid?

The board's chemists are a young but combative bunch, marshalled by the chief flying-chemist, Tony Kallend. They revel in the complexities of their topic. Their critics say that however good their science their real political role is to muddy the waters and confuse. Fred Last at the Institute of Terrestrial Ecology says: 'I see no point in their coming to conferences and talking for an hour about how complicated it all is. Science has to be about simplifying and explaining things.'

There are two main ways in which pollution gases may be converted to acid: the old way and the new way. Chemically, what happens is that extra atoms of oxygen are added to the gases in a process called oxidation. This will not happen on its own in pure air. It requires a triggering chemical. The 'old' way this happens, especially in air heavily polluted with smoke, involves a metal catalyst. Iron and manganese turn up in large quantities in old-style smogs and seem to do the job best. Scientists in Sheffield recently collected rain downwind of a coke works that had a pH of 2.0.[7]

The 'new' way involves the exotic band of photo-oxidants, including ozone. Photo-oxidants turn up even in 'clean' air. Certainly, there are plenty over the North Sea. The chemistry of how these photo-oxidants convert sulphur dioxide to sulphuric acid and nitrogen dioxide to nitric acid is un-utterably complicated. Suffice to say that the generating board's experts hold that ozone is the most important oxidant for sulphur dioxide,[8] while other experts in Britain and the

USA almost all argue for hydrogen peroxide. According to Stuart Penkett of the University of East Anglia, Britain's leading authority, hydrogen peroxide seems to be especially important in clouds or fog where, it now seems, most of the oxidation of sulphur dioxide actually takes place.[9]

Until recently, nobody knew there was any hydrogen peroxide in clouds. And its only widely appreciated use was in turning hair to peroxide blonde. Now diligent atmospheric chemists are finding it everywhere. Wherever acid is formed hydrogen peroxide seems to be around. If it is so important, the obvious question is, would governments be better off trying to cut hydrogen peroxide in the air than in cutting sulphur and nitrogen? The problem is nobody has any clear idea about how to go about doing such a thing, still less about whether it would work. A second question arises: is the production of acid rain limited by the amount of sulphur dioxide in the air or the amount of hydrogen peroxide? The answer may be a bit of both. Because its own creation requires sunlight, there is more hydrogen peroxide around in summer than in winter – six times more over Europe, some scientists say. We know that less acid is created over Europe in winter, but it is more like a sixth less than six times less, so peroxide cannot be that important. Maybe other oxidants, such as ozone, are important in winter, suggests Penkett. It might even be ammonia, another potent oxidant that seems to be everywhere.

It is all a dreadful maze in which new pathways that may or may not lead to the exit are found with bewildering frequency. Even Kallend's flying chemists say they may be losing track. A simpler way forward is to forget the detail of the maze. Instead, why not stand back and look at what goes into the maze and what comes out. That, after all, is what policy-makers need to know.

In September 1983 the generating board's scientists published two papers on acid rain. One was from the flying chemists and it described a plume from Eggborough that did not disperse and in which oxidation was extremely slow.[6] The moral was clear: if money had been spent cleaning up this plume it would have been wasted. The second report was by the generating board's Bernie Fisher and Peter Clark. It may have ruffled feathers inside the board's research laboratories at Leatherhead in Surrey because it crucially undermined the political, if not the scientific, importance of the flying chemists' work.[10]

Fisher and Clark had looked at the available data about sulphur emissions and depositions in Europe and wrote a mathematical model which concluded that what went up came down, and that if you put less up you got less down again. All the hot air about hydrogen peroxide didn't seem to make much difference. To test the model, they took out all the European data from the equations and plugged in some very different figures for emissions in North America. They crossed their fingers and waited to see if the computer would disgorge figures for depositions that matched reality. It did. The two men had, with great elegance, virtually proved their model correct, and with it demonstrated that the simple person's notions about pollution were, in this case, right. Clark explains: 'Whatever the vagaries of the various mechanisms, we know that once sulphur dioxide gets into clouds it is very efficiently removed.'

Some chemical, perhaps one not yet spotted by the chemists, seems always to convert the gas in clouds to acid rain. One day, the flying chemists may find out precisely how this happens. They may well conclude that cutting car exhausts or even turning down the slurry spray would reduce the acidity of rain. But meanwhile, we can be pretty certain that cutting emissions of sulphur dioxide will do the job.

More concrete evidence is also at hand, thanks to Margaret Thatcher. In the first four years of monetarist, Thatcherite Britain, economic recession saw a 25-per-cent reduction in the amount of sulphur dioxide put into the atmosphere by power stations and industry. Over the same years, a series of monitoring sites across Scotland and northern England found a fall in the acid in rain of up to 50 per cent.[11] Across the North Sea in Norway, there has been a very similar reduction in the amount of acid arriving on south-westerly winds from Britain. With other pollutants holding more or less steady over the same period, the evidence that cutting sulphur emissions really does cut sulphur deposition hundreds of kilometres away seems increasingly strong.

The last serious, smoky smog in London was in the winter of 1975. The first, and so far still the worst, of the new photochemical smogs came the following summer. The change of pollution environment was, of course, more gradual than that. But it has been profound. Cars are the new polluters, kicking out ever increasing amounts of hydrocarbons and nitrogen oxides. The result is three times as much nitrate in air and rain as thirty years ago, and perhaps twice as much ozone.

We have not simply swapped one pollutant for another, however. The change is far more subtle – and potentially rather dangerous. Smoke did its damage intensely, but usually locally. So in the old days, did sulphur. Also, smoke obliterated sunlight, and so kept to a minimum the photochemical reactions on which much of the new car-created pollution hinges.

In today's largely smoke-free world, sulphur spreads much further. And with more sunlight there is more chance for photochemical reactions to get going. More photochemistry means more ozone and hydrogen peroxide in the air and, quite probably, some increase in the speed of acid formation in clouds. There is, says Stuart Penkett, 'an increase in chemical reactivity in the atmosphere'.

During the 1960s and 1970s rain became more acid almost everywhere. In the southern Pennines, which have been racked by pollution for 200 years, rain is much more acid than in the 1950s. As acid rain has forced its way into the north of Scotland in recent decades, so ozone pollution is now following. Today there is more pollution than ever before. It is chemically much more reactive. And its reach has extended from the industrial heartlands of the continent to the most remote corners. There are no refuges. Nowhere is untainted.

The great consolation, indeed the great boast of the polluters, is that the old pollution 'hotspots' have gone. The foul, smoke-filled air of yesterday is now rarely found outside

Eastern Europe. Black smogs are gone from London and there are, at any rate sometimes, blue skies over the Ruhr. Visibility in cities has improved, especially in winter. But summer hazes – formed from acid particles hanging in the air, especially when there is plenty of ozone around – have cut visibility in most of Europe in the past three decades. And there are new dangers. We see them in the death of trees in central Europe. Could people be next? To find out, scientists are heading for remote hilltops. On these cold, windswept outposts, where clouds regularly hug the contours, they can investigate what is happening in cloud droplets. This appears to be where the fast chemical reactions that create acid rain are taking place. Much of the most important work is being done in the USA. But first, let us look at what has been uncovered in Britain, the main centre of European research.

The first stop is beside the Chew reservoir, 500 metres up in the south Pennines, east of Manchester. Here the generating board's scientists spent three weeks in 1983 collecting the contents of clouds. They found that when the wind blew from the east, the pH of water droplets in the flat stratus clouds spreading over the bleak hilltop monitoring-point never got above 2.9.[12] To the east, upwind, several of the generating board's largest power stations are lined up less than fifty kilometres away. The lowest pH the scientists measured was 2.5. This is not as acid as some of the worst London smogs, but it is ten times more acid than any rain in the Pennines. The cloud also contained large amounts of metals such as aluminium and titanium, and many particles of fly ash – an indication of the importance of the power stations in forming the acid Pennine fog.

Two trips over Britain by the generating board's flying chemists also show that power station plumes can create massive amounts of acid inside clouds. During a flight in March 1981, tracking a plume from Eggborough, they found that '55 to 60 per cent of the sulphur in the plume was removed in its passage over the cloud-covered south Pennines.'[12] The sulphur dioxide in the plume had been converted to acid in the clouds. The acid had then been deposited on to the ground — not by rain, but by the acid cloud droplets attaching themselves to trees and other vegetation as the clouds engulfed the hillsides.

The second flight, a year later, found that when there was no cloud, much less sulphur was deposited over the south Pennines from the Eggborough plume. The rate of fallout, largely from sulphur dioxide gas being absorbed on the ground, was 6 per cent per hour. But later the same day the plume passed through the clouds covering the north Wales mountains. The plane was there too, and recorded the rate of deposition at 22 per cent. Clouds are where the acid action is to be found.

Scientists from the University of Manchester's Institute of Science and Technology have for fifteen years been running a research station to test atmospheric chemistry on top of Great Dunfell, the second-highest peak in the Pennines. It is close to the Scottish border on the Pennine Way. Since 1983, research here has concentrated on acid fog. Monitors recorded a pH as low as 2.2 in one of the regular 'cap clouds' that surround the peak. Cloud droplets are typically ten or even a hundred times more acid than rain itself.

The investigators believe that what they are seeing is acid rain in a very concentrated form. Before falling out of clouds as rain, these droplets will grow several times over by accumulating clean water vapour, and so diluting the acid and pollutants. Hilltops immersed in cloud are exposed to direct doses of this highly concentrated acid pollution. If cities were built on these hilltops, deadly smogs of the kind that once afflicted London once or twice a decade would happen regularly. That is never likely to happen, however, since they are usually extremely inhospitable places.

Could the processes that create such terrifyingly acid clouds on hilltops also create killer fogs at ground level? Some scientists in the USA believe they could. In August 1984 an acid fog with a pH of less than 3 covered several thousand square kilometres down the eastern seaboard of the USA. Levels of ozone were high, too.[13] Los Angeles has become known as the ozone capital of the world because of its notorious photochemical smogs. It now seems that

Californian fogs, which roll in on cool evening breezes and offer a welcome relief to Californians, are also heavily polluted – but with acid. Los Angeles seems to be the place where the twin pollutants of acid and ozone are beginning to work together in new and worrying ways. Concentrations of metals held close to the ground by the ozone smogs become high enough for the 'old' pollution processes of catalysis to work in tandem with the 'new' processes of photo-oxidation. We have the potential for a killer smog, combining some of the worst features of the old smoke smogs and the new ozone smogs.

When the smoky smog of 1952 killed 4,000 Londoners it had a pH of about 1.6. In December 1982, thirty years almost to the day after London's disaster, Michael R. Hoffmann, a professor of environmental engineering at the prestigious California Institute of Technology, took a sample of fog from Corona del Mar, an isolated spot in California close to the sea and the Mexican border. It had a pH of 1.7.[14] This was the most acid of a series of very acid fogs discovered by Hoffmann and his team during measurements in residential areas and farms as well as close to airports, roads and power stations. In California, it seems, fogs with a pH of less than 3 are regular. And most, says Hoffmann, contain high concentrations of other pollutants such as iron and manganese, which are both efficient catalysts for acid formation.

Hoffmann says that acid fogs and photochemical smogs can feed off each other to devastating effect. The process works like this. First, a summertime ozone smog forms. In this soup of photo-oxidants, the traditional polluting gases, sulphur dioxide and nitrogen oxides, are oxidized to sulphate and nitrate particles, which hang in the air. With no rain to remove them, they stay and accumulate, forming an acid haze of the kind seen all over Europe and the industrial parts of the USA on hot, sunny, ozone-rich days.

As the sun sets and the temperature drops, however, California's coastal fogs form. Fogs form fastest when there are particles in the air on which the droplets can coalesce. In the bad old days, smoke did the job. In the bad new days it is likely to be the sulphate and nitrate particles left over from the previous day's photochemical smog. The droplets that form will be concentrated solutions of sulphuric and nitric acid. The next morning, as the fog evaporates, the acidity of the droplets will reach a peak concentration. And when the fog is gone, the sulphate and nitrate particles remain, ready to mix with the new day's output of pollutants to make a yet thicker haze and a yet more acid fog the next night. Hoffmann expects that dew and even frost could also be extremely acid when there are ozone smogs around.

All this happens in a state where the rain itself has a pH of around 4.8, rather less acid than in remote Scottish highlands. Hoffmann's theories have caused such concern in California that the state's government has set aside $18 million to investigate further – that is five times the entire annual budget from the British government for the whole spectrum of acid-rain research. The state's scientists will investigate whether acid plays a role in the serious damage seen among trees on mountain slopes in the Los Angeles area. As Hoffmann says: 'It is hard to believe that an entire tree bathed in water of about pH 2.5 will fare well.'

Money will also go to investigate the effect of acid fogs on human lungs. Hoffmann himself believes it could do serious damage – even without the masses of black soot that exacerbated problems in the London smogs. California just could be on the verge of a major public health disaster, he says. And where California goes today, the rest of America and Europe follow.

6 Smoke-Filled Rooms

Guilty Parties

The British government's investigators were unequivocal. 'Sulphur dioxide is one of the most harmful of all the polluting agents.' They had been told that a 'promising' process for washing the gas out of emissions from power stations had been 'under consideration for a number of years'. But the electricity authorities were only then considering it for a large-scale trial at a power station. The investigators reported: 'We are not impressed by the speed with which these matters have been pursued. There should be less hesitation about bringing it into practical operation.' It would certainly add to electricity bills, but, the investigators said: 'In our view the cost of gas washing may well be justified by the advantages of a cleaner atmosphere and the human and material benefits that will follow.'

It reads like a polite version of what a House of Commons committee said at the end of 1984 about the Central Electricity Generating Board's attitude to cleaning up acid rain. In fact, it was written in 1954. The recommendation that the generating board's predecessor, the British Electricity Authority, should clean up sulphur dioxide at the same time as it cleaned up smoke pollution, was a central finding of the Beaver report, commissioned in the aftermath of the London smog of 1952.[1]

The pilot study of a form of gas scrubbing known as the Simon-Carves Ammonia process went ahead at the North Wilford power station three years later, in 1957. It was the fourth, and so far last, device for removing sulphur from power station emissions to be installed in Britain. The other three were all in London: at Bankside opposite St Paul's

Cathedral, at Fulham and at Battersea. The Battersea plant, introduced in 1933, was the first, the largest and survived the longest. When Battersea power station closed in 1983, it was for the moment the end for Britain's faltering, half-hearted efforts at sulphur removal.

Britain invented the process, known as flue gas desulphurization (FGD) back in the nineteenth century. When I visited the first West German power station to fit FGD, they took great amusement in handing me a copy of a German article, dated 1880, describing a new British FGD process and successful trials at a power plant in Manchester. But, in a well-established pattern, Britain failed to exploit the discovery. As W. S. Kyte, a chemical engineer based at the generating board's research laboratories, laconically told a conference at the end of 1985: 'The early British work of FGD has been extended in the USA, Japan and West Germany and there are now many FGD plants installed in these countries.'[2] By 1988, 80 per cent of German power stations will have FGD fitted.

There is today a huge world market for FGD equipment which Britain, by being too concerned with the cost of developing and fitting such equipment at home, has lost the chance to exploit. Instead, the giant British engineering firm NEI has done a deal with Mitsubishi, the Japanese firm, to modify its equipment for a British power station. NEI hopes to install it at one of the three power stations set to be fitted with FGD in the 1990s.

The electricity industry came very close to being required to fit FGD to all new power stations more than thirty years ago. But, as Leslie Reed, a former head of the government's air-pollution inspectorate, told MPs in 1983: 'When it came to the post-war expansion and rebuilding of the UK power industry, the inspectorate considered that it was impracticable to require sulphur-dioxide removal from the very much larger boiler plants then being built.'[3] The inspectorate settled instead for tall chimneys to disperse the gas. Even so, since 1948, all new British power stations have, as a condition of planning approval, been required to set aside land for FGD equipment. Until 1986, this requirement had never been drawn on.

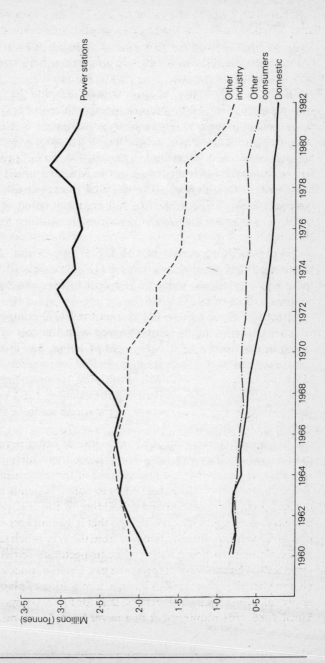

Sources of British sulphur dioxide emissions since 1960

Millions (Tonnes)

3·5
3·0
2·5
2·0
1·5
1·0
0·5

1960 1962 1964 1966 1968 1970 1972 1974 1976 1978 1980 1982

Power stations

Other industry

Other consumers

Domestic

A Change of Mind

One of the interesting features of Margaret Thatcher's administration in the mid-1980s has been the emergence of a green hue within the government. The banner is carried by a young 'blue-chip' Tory, William Waldegrave. He has borne the reputation of being 'a future prime minister' for several years, and during a longish tenure as a minister within the Department of the Environment he contrived to make parts of it appear like a department concerned with the environment. Even the letterhead changed from brown to green. A group of clandestinely green scientists at the department has stepped, bleary-eyed, from the closet. At their head, egging Waldegrave on, is the department's chief scientist, Martin Holdgate.

Sometime in the early 1980s Holdgate's scientists became convinced that Norwegian claims about acid rain were right and the righteous warnings from the generating board about scientific uncertainties were largely prevarication. Insiders put the date of conversion at June 1982, when scientists from the department attended a 'think'tank' in Stockholm prior to a ministerial conference on acid rain. I went too and reported afterwards in *New Scientist* magazine:

British researchers and civil servants returned from [the] conference convinced that acid rain poses a real threat to forests and woodlands throughout Britain. In the next few weeks, they will tell ministers that it would be in Britain's interest to cut emissions of sulphur from fossil-fuelled power stations. And they will press for bigger grants to study the effects of airborne sulphur on soil and plant growth.[4]

Bob Wilson, one of the department's scientists there, told me that he had been convinced that acid rain was no longer a matter of a 'few Norwegian lakes'. Wilson now runs a much-increased research budget for acid rain at the department. But twice, in 1984 and 1985, the department lost battles on Cabinet committees when it tried to translate science into action. The battles were over whether Britain should join the '30 per cent club' of nations, including most of western Europe, committed to reducing their sulphur emissions by 30 per cent from 1980 levels. It is widely said that the second defeat should have been a victory. The Foreign Secretary, Geoffrey Howe, had the deciding vote. His departmental brief was to assuage the diplomatic pressure from Norway and vote for joining the club. This he did not do. Sober mandarins from the environment department insist that the generating board engineered the débâcle through Lord Marshall's 'close contacts' with the prime minister. After that, the gloves were off. Marshall authorized the spending of a cool £300,000 on a half-hour 'educational' video film about acid rain. The film angered the Norwegians so much that their prime minister complained about it at an acrimonious summit meeting with Margaret Thatcher. The Norwegian Embassy brought its top scientists to a press conference in London to explain their anger. The video 'concealed and twisted facts'; they said. Even the generating board's scientists discreetly let it be known that they were annoyed by the final version of the video. They wondered aloud why the film blamed tree planting for acidifying lakes above the tree-line. They already knew that the board was on a losing wicket and would eventually be forced to concede the scientific case.

The environment department called in journalists before Christmas 1985 to 'dissociate' itself from the film, which gave 'a selective account of the scientific arguments'. The film 'attempts to minimize the British contribution to acid deposition in Norway when it is much the largest', the department said. Waldegrave followed this up by announcing that he and the Norwegians agreed that Britain was causing acid rain to Norway, and he praised the Norwegians for the 'model way' in which they had conducted their campaign against Britain's polluters.

When, in the summer of 1986, Waldegrave finally persuaded the prime minister and Lord Marshall to accept the need for action on acid rain, it was an important feather in his cap. He had caught a growing political tide of concern about 'green' issues in Britain, coupled with the Foreign Office's worries over its relations with Norway (a trusted

NATO ally) and the prime minister's concern to smooth her way to re-election for a third term.

But it was, in reality, a very small victory. As the Whitehall battle raged, the Department of Energy prepared new predictions of future energy demand which implied increases in sulphur emissions from Britain's power stations of up to 30 per cent by the end of the century. This would cancel out a reduction of some 25 per cent in emissions between 1980 and 1985 which resulted in large part from industrial recession. Future predictions of energy demand are notoriously unreliable, but the projections made nonsense of the government's expressed intention, 'as an act of policy', to ensure that sulphur emissions continued to fall.

Marshall announced in late 1986 that his programme to fit FGD to three large power stations by 1997 would 'ensure that our emissions of sulphur dioxide continue to decline through the remainder of this century'. This was no less than the truth. It was just that it had been hoped all along to do this without installing FGD. After Marshall's announcement, Waldegrave's staff admitted that Britain was still not in a position to join the '30 per cent club' with any certainty of meeting the terms of membership.

Beyond the '30 per cent club', however, there was, in late 1986, a new threat on the horizon that seemed likely, eventually, to force the CEGB to take much more radical steps to cut its pollution. The battle was over a proposal from the European Community to force much larger cuts in emissions of sulphur from power stations. Plans for a forced 60 per cent cut were dropped in March 1986. But at that time, Britain remained the only nation among the twelve not in favour of some form of '30 per cent plus' directive.

The new, green Department of the Environment wants to shed Britain's image as 'the dirty man of Europe', but it is forced by other departments to oppose measures that its mandarins and scientists alike want to support. Meanwhile, most other European countries are forging ahead. Sweden has promised a 60 per cent cut in sulphur emissions by 1995. France plans 50 per cent by 1990, West Germany 50 per cent by 1993, Norway and Denmark 50 per cent by 1995, and so on.

There are three ways of cutting sulphur pollution from a power station. You can do it by burning fuel with less sulphur in it. You can do it with technology that takes out sulphur during burning. By about the end of the century a new technique called 'fluidized bed combustion' may be available to do this. Or you can bolt FGD on to the station chimney.

Most attention has centred on this third option. It is expensive, but it will remove at least 90 per cent of the sulphur. And, at any rate in Germany, you can have one attached to your power plant inside eighteen months. The fluidized bed received rave reviews from the House of Lords' Science and Technology Committee in 1984. But it may turn out to be expensive and will anyway be a little too late to meet the likely requirements of the EEC directive.

Extraordinarily little attention has been given to the possibilities of burning low-sulphur coal. Rather a lot of people have an interest in not mentioning the idea. The coal board would have to admit that Britain's low-sulphur coal (with less than 1 per cent sulphur) is found in Scotland and south Wales, where it is shutting pits as fast as it can. And the government would have to acknowledge that cheap, low-sulphur coal is ready and waiting on the international market, if it were willing to allow the generating board to buy it. Canadian coal supplied to some West German power stations has a sulphur content of 0.3 per cent. If we allow oil back into the argument the ministers would also have to agree that some of the world's least sulphurous oil is on Britain's doorstep, under the North Sea. The problem is that the generating board would rather buy cheap sulphurous oil from the Middle East.

Most British coal is washed at the colliery to remove ash. The washing also removes some sulphur. But the generating board says that more washing would be as expensive a way of removing sulphur as FGD. About half the sulphur in most coals is in the form of iron pyrites. The board is investigating designs of high-powered magnets that could extract the pyrites from powdered coal immediately before it is fed into power-station boilers.[5]

A final possibility would be to burn low-sulphur coal whenever there were a chance of the sulphur raining on to some sensitive location, such as Scotland or Scandinavia. This idea has been examined by the Met Office, which claims an 80 per cent accuracy in predicting whether air passing over, say, Drax power station will eventually pass over Scandinavia. If all Britain's large power stations had two piles of coal – one low-sulphur and one 'regular', then they could switch to the low-sulphur pile on the one day in five when Norway seemed most at risk. According to scientists at the Department of the Environment, 'this could result in a 50 per cent reduction in deposition in southern Norway.'[6]

The chief protagonist of the idea of switching between coal stocks is Barry Smith at the Met Office. He says: 'It was evident to me as early as 1974 that if we could forecast when these episodes would occur . . . then depositions could be significantly reduced.' Recent analysis has shown that there are around twenty occasions each year when significant amounts of British acid fall anywhere in Scandinavia, says Smith. 'If we can forecast occasions of heavy rain successfully, we may not need to be incredibly accurate in our trajectory forecasting.' He believes the job can be done.

July 1985 was a bad month for acid rain in southern Norway. There were seven acid downpours with a pH as low as 3.6. The acid for three of them came from Britain, including two of the worst three episodes.[7] In each case the published weather forecasts predicted the wind direction and the likelihood of rain well in advance. Much of the acid that fell in southern Norway that month could thus have been efficiently and cheaply prevented by Britain.

The problem, as Smith says, is that 'countries other than those in Scandinavia would probably demand the same favoured treatment. Certainly they would object to "dirty" fuel being reserved for airflows passing over themselves.' Clearly, for a switching policy to be tenable, there would have to be no overall increase in the amount of sulphur sent in any particular direction. But it could be an extraordinarily cheap way of cutting acid rain in countries at most risk.

According to Smith, the generating board has been 'rather lukewarm about the idea'. I got that impression, too. This, on the face of it, is rather odd. The board now accepts that its pollution is helping to damage Scandinavian lakes. But it still holds that most of its sulphur falls harmlessly. What matters is whether it lands where it may do harm. Many scientists involved in the acid-rain debate would disagree with this analysis. They would say that all acid emissions are likely, eventually, to do harm. But if the generating board believes it, then the board ought to be trying to end its pollution of Scandinavia as cheaply as possible. Burning low-sulphur coal on days when the Met Office raises its 'acid-warning cones' could have a dramatic impact on British pollution of Scandinavia. The cost of keeping each tonne of sulphur from falling on that sensitive part of the world would be about a fifth that of FGD. And the job could be done very quickly. It is not a substitute for FGD. But it could provide early relief for Scandinavia while a full programme of fitting FGD gets under way. What, one might ask, is the CEGB waiting for?

Cleaning Up the Sulphur

Occasional attempts are made to put a price tag on the damage done by acid rain. But how do you do it? One study estimated the lost productivity of fish stocks in Scandinavia at about $60 million.[8] Another tried to add in a figure for how much Scandinavians valued going fishing. Half a million fishermen in affected areas of Sweden said they would pay $200 a year for the return of the fish – putting a value on the lost opportunity for Swedes to 'go fishing' of up to $100 million.

Some economists say the cost of repairing pollution damage to buildings in Europe is about a billion dollars a year. But how do you value the loss as the Acropolis is eaten away? We must be suspicious that air pollution is still sending asthmatics to hospital, killing vulnerable young babies, shortening the lives of many old people and making us all more susceptible to everything from coughs to chronic bronchitis. How do you cost that, or the splendid view that disappears in a haze on hot, sunny, ozone-rich days?

A study in the USA has put the current extra cost of making car tyres that do not crack under the impact of ozone at perhaps $500 million a year.[9] Ozone damage to crops is put at four times that. But how do you measure the cost of ozone's assault on the pigment of irreplaceable paintings?

British consultants have told the EEC that emission controls costing £5 billion might bring benefits worth only half that, but it left out of the equation damage to buildings and human health. There is undoubtedly a tenable economic case for reducing air pollution, leaving aside ecological, aesthetic or humanitarian matters. The overwhelming evidence is that all the pollutants we have discussed are harmful and that, together, they have more serious effects than singly. The only real solution is to start cutting them all.

In Europe, given the will to do anything at all, there are two ways of proceeding to reduce sulphur pollution. One, which most European countries have opted for by joining the '30 per cent club', is to set an overall target for reductions in emissions. Every country aims to meet the target, regardless of how much pollution they produce now, where their pollution falls or how much demonstrable harm it does.

A second, more subtle, approach would be to set targets for the maximum amount of deposition of pollution allowed outside urban areas. Then sophisticated models of the movement of pollution could be used to set different targets for different countries' emissions.

Such an approach was suggested by Sweden at the conference on acid rain in Stockholm in 1982. The Swedish government argued that serious damage seemed to begin in Scandinavia when sulphur deposition rose above 0.5 grams per square metre per year. So that figure could be set as the maximum allowable deposition anywhere. In Stockholm, the idea was hounded from the final report of the think-tank by scientists from Britain and the USA. The generating board's Gwyneth Howells, always a formidable debater, argued long and hard that such a limit implied an 80 per cent cut in emissions. So be it, replied the Swedes.[4]

The idea of deposition targets is still around. Dick Wright, the American in Oslo, points out that all the damage to the environment that we know about from acid rain in Europe occurs where the average pH of rain is less than 4.7. So maybe one target should be to get everywhere above that level. The sensitivity of environments to acid varies so much that deposition limits would still be a crude tool. Nevertheless after the blanket reductions of the '30 per cent club', they should be the next step. However, at the end of 1986, the European Community remained unable to agree on any plan to cut emissions across the board – let alone one based on the needs of sensitive environments.

International pressure has yet to make much impact on the three grossest polluters in Eastern Europe – Poland, East Germany and Czechoslovakia. But there, as in Britain in the 1950s, local damage from acid fallout is so intense that self-interest will probably be the first spur to action. In late 1985 Czechoslovakia declared its industrial heartland of northern Bohemia an ecological and public-health disaster area and promised to pour vast funds into cleaning up the worst environmental excesses.[10]

The cash commitment of the governments of western Europe to reducing their sulphur emissions is now considerable. Soon Europe's politicians will ask scientists for signs that it has been well spent. They will want to see lakes full of fish and revitalized forests. Some scientists believe they will get them quickly. They point to the rising pH in reservoirs in the industrial Pennines of England in recent years, for instance, and early signs of recovery in Sweden. They expect that recent reductions in the deposition of sulphur in Scotland and parts of Norway will quickly be reflected in less acid lakes and a return of fish. Dick Wright has predicted that 'a 30-per-cent reduction in sulphur deposition will restore chemical conditions such that 22 per cent of the lakes now experiencing fisheries problems should be able to support fish'.[11] But that was before his latest experiments in Norway showed evidence of the extent of acid and sulphur accumulated in Scandinavian soils.

Others warn against expecting too much, too soon. As we have seen Britain's scientists say that a 50-per-cent reduction in emissions is needed to stop upland waters becoming more acid. Hans Seip, Wright's Norwegian comrade in arms, warns that 'it is reasonable to believe that soils may become still more acidic at the present levels of deposition.'[12] He fears, like the Britons, that 'deposition would have to be reduced by more than 50 per cent to bring the brown trout back' to upland streams. Martin Holdgate, the chief scientist at Britain's Department of the Environment and architect of the greening of that department, goes further. He issued a telling warning during a conference on acid rain at the Royal Society in London in 1983. 'We have only begun to glimpse the time scales involved in these phenomena,' he said. 'There is evidence that some changes, in catchments and forest soils alike, are slow, and have been operating for decades if not centuries. Many are unlikely to be rapidly reversible. There is a disturbing implication that whatever measures we take – even if we know enough to manipulate the most sensitive variables, which many scientists doubt – we may have to wait years or even decades for the signs of improvement to appear.'[13] This is not a counsel of despair – still less an argument for doing nothing. Holdgate is appalled at the extent to which Europeans have abused their continent's most complex and vulnerable ecological systems.

For all the current signs of imaginative engagement by some European politicians in matters green, Holdgate's is a long time-scale for them. Waldegrave might be a greying prime minister before the fish come back to Galloway. But if nothing is done to reduce sulphur emissions, he may be off to see the Queen rather sooner – to explain why the fish have disappeared from the lochs of her Balmoral estate.

An Autobahn into the Future

It is all but certain that by the 1990s, nitrogen will be top of the list of Europe's air pollutants. If we knew as much about it as we know about sulphur it might be there already. As the power stations are cleaned up the car is set to supersede them as the single most deadly agent of air pollution.

The case against cars is this. In recent years they have

become the biggest source of nitrogen oxides in the atmosphere over Europe. In most towns and cities they are pushing concentrations of nitrogen dioxide near major roads towards levels which are clearly dangerous. And they are ensuring that, over most of Europe today, whether town or country, there is as much nitrogen in the air as sulphur. Nitric acid is sometimes as important in acid rain as sulphuric acid, especially in winter when conversion of sulphur dioxide to acid is slower than in summer. In many places, soils are becoming saturated with nitrates, which are joining sulphates in rivers and groundwaters.

In addition, nitrogen oxides are an essential component in the formation of ozone, hydrogen peroxide and the other photo-oxidants. The other essential components for the formation of photo-oxidants are reactive hydrocarbons. Cars are today the biggest source of these as well. Among the photo-oxidants, ozone in particular is a major hazard in its own right, threatening human health, crops and perhaps trees on a wide scale. In the next century, it may also pose a threat to the world's climate by producing a 'greenhouse effect' comparable to that from carbon dioxide.

And there is more. If photo-oxidants do turn out to be the main agent for oxidizing sulphur dioxide to sulphuric acid inside clouds, then, once more, cars may take the blame for much of the extra damage that sulphur emissions have been doing in the past three decades.

None of this lets power stations off the hook. It is they that produce most of the sulphur dioxide, as well as a third or more of the nitrogen oxides in countries such as Britain. (This is quite inexcusable, since these nitrogen oxides are very cheap to remove.) The only thing power stations have clean hands over in this deadly pollution merry-go-round is the production of hydrocarbons.

Today, we have equal partners in crime. But as every power station bolts on FGD equipment, so the finger of blame points more firmly to the car. The targets of the environmentalists will be Ford and Mercedes. So what is being done to meet the challenge? In mid-1985, the European Community agreed on a directive under which most of its member states will fit devices called catalytic converters to the exhaust pipes of larger cars. These converters remove a proportion of the carbon monoxide, hydrocarbons and nitrogen oxides from the exhausts' gases. But Britain's Department of Transport says Britain's pollution from cars has not increased in recent years and it has refused point-blank to have anything to do with the converters. Since the EEC directive in this case is only 'permissive', there is nothing that Britain's partners can do to force Britain to act.

The British decision evidently irritated Waldegrave at the Department of the Environment. But he doggedly perseveres with the argument that a new generation of 'lean-burn' engines being developed in Britain and elsewhere will allow Britain to reduce its emissions by the 1990s. 'Lean-burn' engines burn fuel in a mixture rich in air. They should save fuel as well as cutting pollution from nitrogen oxides. In fact, lean-burn engines only cut out nitrogen oxides, not the hydrocarbons pinpointed by British scientists as the key factor in ozone smogs. So a simplified catalyst would be needed anyway for lean burn, making a nonsense of Britain's principle stand against catalysts.

At the end of 1986 this was academic as Denmark used its veto. It wants to impose the same tough emission standards on small cars as the directive allows for large cars, and it was refusing to agree unless it was changed to allow this.

Europe's problems from car pollution will not go away with the new directive. The directive will take years to implement, since it only applies to new cars. And, as fast as the pollution from individual journeys by car drops, the number of journeys driven will rise. Current predictions are that the directive will cut emissions of nitrogen oxides from cars by about 30 per cent by the year 2000. But this will be more than cancelled out because traffic volumes are predicted to rise by anything between 25 and 50 per cent.

Germany has 25 millions cars, and a system of autobahns to match. Some 80 per cent of German traffic is on the autobahn, compared with 20 per cent of British traffic on motorways. The man at the research ministry in Bonn put his problem succinctly: 'Our autobahn network is designed for driving fast.' Cars driven fast kick out more nitrogen oxides. The German speed limit is 130 kilometres per hour (a little more than 80 miles per hour), but is widely ignored. Many prosperous Germans live in houses near the country's forests and drive long distances to their city offices. They drive past sick trees every day, but are barely aware that their speed may be helping to kill the trees.

Scientists at the Heidelberg Institute for Energy and Environment Research say that a lower speed limit of 100 kilometres per hour (62 mph) could overnight cut emissions of nitrogen oxides from cars by 20 per cent. In a rare chance to put the boot on the other foot, Waldegrave told British MPs in January 1985: 'It would help us all if the Germans tackled the problem of their speed limits.' That month, the German government began an experiment. It imposed a speed limit of 100 kilometres per hour on twenty sections of autobahns across the country and waited to see what happened. It measured the speed of cars and how much emissions of pollution changed.

A year later nobody seemed too sure about the results. They appear to have shown only a limited reduction in emissions – largely because few Germans obeyed the new speed limit. The issue of whether the limit should be adopted nationally got bogged down in politics. The Federal Environment Agency wanted speed limits. But the Chancellor, Helmut Kohl, had come to power promising not to impose them. The official line in Bonn is that 'reductions in speeds would not make a big contribution'. This is humbug. More to the point, the man in the ministry says: 'Speed limits would reduce the number of German cars made. People would buy a Datsun, not a Porsche.'

In Switzerland, where all new cars will have to be fitted with catalysts after October 1987, even the sight of mountainsides full of sick fir trees could not persuade the government to accept a plan to lower speed limits from 120 to 100 kilometres per hour. In two of the richest countries in Europe, with the two most serious problems of dying trees, the freedom of the autobahn has won out over the national love of trees.

This book began with an image of London in December

1952. Darkness at noon; a capital paralysed by its own pollution; the mortuaries filling with the victims. It was the summit of the old pollution, at the hub of an empire on the verge of dissolution. Today, the economic centre of Europe has moved south to southern Germany, to cities such as Munich and Stuttgart, and to Switzerland. The air there is free of smoke. By the 1990s, the sulphur will be diminished. But, charged with photo-oxidants, the air will be among the most chemically active in Europe. Its mists, hanging in the Black Forest close to Stuttgart, will probably be as acid as any in California. The acid will be from nitrogen, blowing off the autobahns, rather than from sulphur. And in summer the ozone will reach record levels, spreading out to cast a new pall of pollution across Europe. The skies will be blue (if a little hazy). But they will still be poisoned.

Notes

1 A Pall over Europe

1. *The Times*, 8 December 1952
2. 'Mortality and Morbidity During the London Fog of December 1952', *Reports of Public Health and Medical Subjects No. 95*, Ministry of Health, 1954
3. *The Times*, 6 December 1952
4. *The Times*, 8 December 1952
5. W. C. Brogger, *Naturen*, v. 5, p. 47, 1881
6. K. Dahl, *Salmon and Trout Magazine*, v. 46, pp. 35–43, 1927
7. S. E. Sunde, 'The Acid Rivers of Sorland', *Friskesport*, 2, 1936
8. A. Dannevig, *Jager og Fisker*, v. 3, pp. 116–18, 1959
9. S. Oden, 'The Acidification of Air and Precipitation and its Consequences on the Natural Environment', Swedish National Science Research Council Ecology Committee, 1968
10. 'Der Wald Stirbt', *Der Spiegel*, 16 November 1981
11. B. Ulrich, 'An Ecosystem Oriented Hypothesis on the Effect of Air Pollution on Forest Ecosystems', Paper to Stockholm Conference on the Acidification of the Environment, 1982
12. 1985 Forest Damage Survey, West German Federal Ministry of Food, Agriculture and Forestry
13. D. Fowler, et al., 'The Air Pollution Climate of Non-Nordic Europe', *Water, Air and Soil Pollution*, (in the press)

2 Corroding Gases

1. T. E. Davies, et al., 'Black Acidic Snow in the Remote Scottish Highlands', *Nature*, v. 312, pp. 58–61, 1984
2. John Evelyn, *Fumifugium, A Chemical Climatology*, London, 1661
3. R. A. Smith, *Air and Rain*, Longmans Green & Co., London, 1872

4. Lord Ashby, and M. Anderson, 'The Historical Roots of the British Clean Air Act 1956: III, The Ripening of Public Opinion', *Interdisciplinary Science Reviews*, v. 2, No. 3, 1977

5. Lord Ashby, 'Clean Air Over London', *Clean Air*, National Society for Clean Air, pp. 25–30, Spring 1975

6. J. A. Lee, et al., 'Responses to Acidic Deposition in Ombotrophic Mires', in *Effects of Acidic Deposition and Air Pollutants on Forest Wetlands and Agricultural Ecosystems*, Springer Verlag, Berlin, 1986

7. R. Lines, 'Species and Seed Origin Trials in the Industrial Pennines', *Quarterly Journal of Forestry*, v. 78, pp. 9–23, 1984

8. *The Times*, 12 December 1952

9. *The Times*, 17 December 1952

10. Memorandum to Cabinet, 18 November 1953, quoted by M. Hamer, *New Scientist*, p. 3, 5 January 1984

11. Committee on Air Pollution Report, Cmnd 9322, November 1954

12. D. Laxen and M. Schwar, 'Acid Rain and London', Scientific Services Branch, Greater London Council, 1985

13. D. Laxen, et al., 'Sulphur Dioxide in London's Air', *London Environmental Bulletin*, Scientific Services Branch, Greater London Council, Spring 1985

14. C. F. Barrett, et al., 'Acid Deposition in the United Kingdom', Warren Spring Laboratory, 1983

15. D. Laxen, 'Nitrogen Dioxide: An Air Quality Problem for London?' *London Environmental Bulletin*, Scientific Services Branch, Greater London Council, Autumn 1985

16. British Lichen Society, 'Lichens, Acid Rain and Building Stones, A Statement for the House of Commons Select Committee', July 1984

17. C. I. Rose and D. L. Hawksworth, 'Lichen Recolonization in London's Cleaner Air', *Nature*, v. 289, pp. 289–92, 1981

18. O. Gilbert, 'Field Evidence for an Acid Rain Effect on Lichens', *Environmental Pollution (Series A)*, v. 40, pp. 227–31, 1986

19. L. Timberlake, 'Poland – The Most Polluted Country in the World?', *New Scientist*, 22 October 1981

20. J. Rostowski, 'Environmental Deterioration in Poland', Radio Free Europe Research Report, 5 September 1984

21. M. Morawska-Horawska, 'Cloudiness and Sunshine in Cracow, 1861–1980', *Journal of Climatology*, v. 5, pp. 633–42, 1985

22. Radio Free Europe Research Report, 31 December 1983

23. S. J. Kabala, 'Poland: Facing the Hidden Costs of Development', *Environment*, November 1985

24. Czechoslovak Academy of Sciences, 'An Analysis of the Ecological Situation in Czechoslovakia', *Listy*, 1984. Reviewed by Andrew Csepel in 'Czechs and the (cological Balance', *New Scientist*, 27 September 1984

25. B. V. Flow, 'Environmental Crisis in the GDR', Radio Free Europe Research Report, 3 September 1984

26. B. Komarov, *The Destruction of Nature in the Soviet Union*, Pluto Press, London, 1978

27. B. T. Commins, et al., *Atmospheric Environment*, v. 1, pp. 49–68, 1967

28. R. E. Waller, et al., 'Clean Air and Health in London', Proceedings of Clean Air Conference, National Society for Clean Air, 1969

29. M. J. Gardner, et al., *Atlas of Mortality for Selected Diseases in England and Wales 1968–78*, John Wiley, Chichester, 1984

30. W. W. Holland and D. D. Reid, 'The Urban Factor in Chronic Bronchitis', *Lancet*, pp. 445–8, 1965

31. J. E. Lunn, et al., 'Patterns of Respiratory Illness in Sheffield Infant Schoolchildren', *British J Prev Soc Med*, v. 21, pp. 7–16, 1967

32. J. W. B. Douglas and R. S. Waller, 'Air Pollution and Respiratory Infections in Children', *British J Prev Soc Med*, v. 20, pp. 1–8, 1966

33. T. V. Larson, et al., 'Ammonia in Human Airways, Neutralization of Inspired Acid Sulphate Aerosols', *Science*, v. 197, pp. 161–3, 1977

34. M. R. Hoffmann, *Environmental Science and Technology*, v. 18, pp. 61–3, 1984

35. D. V. Bates, *The Strength of the Evidence Relating Air Pollutants to Adverse Health Effects*, Institute for Environmental Studies, University of North Carolina, Chapel Hill, 1984

36. M. Hazucha and D. V. Bates, 'Combined Effects of Ozone and Sulphur Dioxide on Human Pulmonary Function', *Nature*, v. 257, pp. 50–1, 1975

37. T. N. Skoulikidis, 'Effects of Primary and Secondary Air Pollutants and Acid Depositions on (Ancient and Modern) Buildings and Monuments', Paper to Symposium on Acid Deposition: A Challenge for Europe, Commission of the European Communities, Karlsruhe, September 1983

38. M. Del Monte, et al., 'Urban Stone Sulphation and Oil-fired

Carbonaceous Particles', *The Science of the Total Environment*, v. 36, pp. 369–76, 1984

39. G. Thomson, *The Museum Environment*, Butterworths, London, 1978

40. House of Commons Environment Committee: Acid Rain, July 1984. Much of the subsequent information in this section comes from written evidence from architects to this committee. The evidence is available at the House of Commons Library

41. Hansard, col. 1011–73, 11 January 1985

42. Robert Porter, Surveyor to the Fabric of St Paul's Cathedral, Evidence to Commons Environmental Committee Inquiry into Acid Rain, 1984

43. A. D. Sharp, et al., 'Weathering of the Balustrade on St Paul's Cathedral, London', *Earth Surface Processes and Landforms*, v. 7, pp. 387–9, 1982

44. R. N. Butlin, and R. V. Cooke, 'Research on Limestone Decay in the UK', Proceedings of International Symposium of Stone Decay and Conservation, Lausanne, 1985

45. R. N. Butlin, 'Further Perspectives on Acid Rain – Effects of Acid Deposition on UK Buildings', Paper to annual conference of National Society for Clean Air, 1985

46. J. F. Feenstra, 'Cultural Property and Air Pollution', Ministry of Housing, Physical Planning and Environment, Netherlands, 1984

47. R. Cheng, 'Emissions from Electric Power Plants and their Impact on the Environment', in *Energy, Resources and Environment*, Pergamon Press, Oxford, 1983

48. R. J. Schaffer, 'The Weathering of Natural Building Stone', Building Research Special Report No. 18, DSIR, 1932

49. I. Peterson, 'A Material Loss', Report on conference of American Chemical Society, *Science News*, 7 September 1985

50. G. Frenzel, 'The Restoration of Medieval Stained Glass', *Scientific American*, 1985

51. House of Commons Environment Committee, Follow-up to the Environment Committee Report on Acid Rain, Appendix 3: Letter from Professor Newton, 1985

52. G. M. A. Jones, Water Research Centre, personal communication, 1985

53. National Economic Development Council, Investment in the Public Sector Built Infrastructure, 1985

54. P. G. Clark, 'The Cost of Quality', *Water*, National Water Council, September 1981

55. F. Pearce, *Watershed*, Junction Books, London, 1982

56. T. R. Shaw, 'Corrosion Map of the British Isles', American Society for Testing and Materials, 1978

57. J. P. Chilton, 'The Corrosion of Metals', *Journal of the Royal Society of Arts*, August 1971

58. Report of the Committee on Corrosion and Protection, Department of Trade and Industry, 1971

59. Correspondence held by Friends of the Earth, London, 1985

3 Acid Waters

1. S. E. Sunde, Annual Report of the Fishery Inspector to the Norwegian Department of Agriculture, 1926

2. A. Henriksen, et al., 'Episodic Changes in pH and Aluminium-speciation Kill Fish in a Norwegian Salmon River', *Vatten* 40, pp. 255–60, 1984

3. R. Andersen, et al., 'Effects of Acidification on Age Class Composition in Arctic Char and Brown Trout in a Coastal Area, SW Norway', Institute of Freshwater Research Report 61, National Swedish Board of Fisheries, 1984

4. G. Howells, 'Acid Waters – the Effect of Low pH and Acid Associated Factors on Fisheries', *Applied Biology*, 1983

5. D. W. Schindler, et al., 'Long-Term Ecosystem Stress: The Effects of Years of Experimental Acidification on a Small Lake', *Science*, v. 228, pp. 1395–1401, 1985

6. Ivan Rosenqvist, 'Acid Precipitation and Other Possible Sources for Acidification of Rivers and Lakes', *Science of the Total Environment*, v. 10, pp. 271–2, 1978

7. Central Electricity Generating Board, Acid Rain (video), 1985

8. R. A. Skeffington, 'Effects of Acid Precipitation and Natural Soil Acidification Processes on Soil', *Journal of the Southeast England Soils Discussion Group*, v. 2, 1986

9. D. J. A. Brown, *Loch Fleet News*, No. 5, Central Electricity Research Laboratories, December 1985

10. Freshwater Fisheries Laboratory, Evidence to House of Commons Environment Committee Inquiry into Acid Rain, 1984

11. Clyde River Purification Board, Annual Report, 1985

12. R. Batterbee and R. Flower, 'Palaeoecological Evidence for the Timing and Causes of Lake Acidification in Galloway, Southwest Scotland', Final Report for the Central Electricity Generating Board, 1985

13. Clyde River Purification Board, 'Acidification of Surface Waters in CRPB Area', Internal Report, November 1983
14. Clyde River Purification Board, Annual Report, 1984
15. North East River Purification Board, Evidence to House of Commons Environment Committee Inquiry into Acid Rain, 1984
16. Freshwater Fisheries Laboratory Triennial Review, 1982–4
17. D. H. Crawshaw, 'The Effects of Acidic Runoff on Streams in Cumbria', North West Water, Internal Report, 1984
18. E. Y. Haworth, 'The Highly Nervous System of the English Lakes', Freshwater Biological Association, Annual Report, 1985
19. W. Pennington, 'Long-Term Natural Acidification of Upland Sites in Cumbria: Evidence from Post-Glacial Lake Sediments', Freshwater Biological Association, Annual Report, 1984
20. V. Jones, et al., 'Lake Acidification and the Land-Use Hypothesis: A Mid-Post-Glacial Analogue', Nature, v. 322, pp. 157–8, 1986
21. A. M. C. Edwards, Yorkshire Water Authority, personal communication, 1986
22. Welsh Water, Report of Working Group on Welsh Salmon and Sea-Trout Fisheries, 1985
23. J. H. Stoner and A. S. Gee, 'Effects of Forestry on Water Quality and Fish in Welsh Rivers and Lakes', Journal of the Institute of Water Engineers and Scientists, v. 39, No. 1, p. 27, 1985
24. Institute of Hydrology, Evidence to House of Commons Environment Committee Inquiry into Acid Rain, 1984
25. Severn Trent Water, Evidence to House of Commons Environment Committee Inquiry into Acid Rain, 1984
26. S. Ormerod and R. W. Edwards, 'Stream Acidity in Some Areas of Wales in Relation to Historical Trends in Afforestation and the Usage of Agricultural Limestone', Journal of Environmental Management, v. 20, pp. 189–97, 1985
27. C. Jordon, Freshwater Biological Investigation Unit, Department of Environment, Northern Ireland, personal communication, 1986
28. C. R. Townsend, A. G. Hildrew and J. Francis, 'Community Structure in some Southern English Streams: the Influence of Physicochemical Factors', Freshwater Biology, v. 13, pp. 521–44, 1983
29. G. L. A. Fry and A. S. Cooke, Acid Deposition and its Implications for Nature Conservation in Britain, Nature Conservancy Council, 1984

30. S. Ormerod and S. J. Tyler, *Birds and Surface-water Acidity: A Critical Review*, in press

31. C. Neal, et al., The Effects of Acidic Deposition and Conifer Afforestation on Stream Acidity in the British Uplands', *Journal of Hydrology*, 1986

32. 'Lake Gardsjon: An Acid Forest Lake and its Catchment', eds. F. Anderson and B. Olsson, Ecological Bulletins 37, Publishing House of the Swedish Research Councils, 1985

33. *Acidification Today and Tomorrow*, Swedish Ministry of Agriculture, study prepared for Stockholm Conference on the Acidification of the Environment, 1982

34. R. F. Wright, 'Acidification of Freshwaters in Europe', *Water Quality Bulletin*, v. 8, pp. 137–42, 1983

35. P. Chester, 'Perspectives on Acid Rain', *Journal of the Royal Society of Arts*, September 1983

36. *The Times*, 8 February 1982

37. European Community Screening Programme for Lead: United Kingdom Results, Department of the Environment

38. M. E. Moore, Proceedings of the Symposium on Toxic Effects of Environmental Lead, Conservation Society, 1979

39. D. G. Wibberley, et al., *Journal of Medical Genetics*, v. 14, p. 339, 1977

40. M. E. Moore, 'Plumbosolvency in Waters', *Nature*, v. 243, pp. 222–3, 1973

41. H. L. Needleman, et al., 'Deficits in Psychologic and Classroom Performance of Children with Elevated Dentine Lead Levels', *New England Journal of Medicine*, v. 300, pp. 689–95, 1979

42. E. L. Baker, et al., 'Occupational Lead Neuro-toxicity: Improvement in Behavioural Effects after Reduction of Exposure', *British Journal of Industrial Medicine*, v. 42, pp. 507–16, 1985

43. 'Lead in Tapwater: A Menace for Millions', p.9, *New Scientist*, 29 November 1984

44. S. J. Pocock, et al., 'British Regional Heart Study: Geographical Variations in Cardiovascular Mortality and the Role of Water Quality', *British Medical Journal*, v. 280, pp. 1243–9, 1980

45. W. R. Harlan, et al., 'Blood Lead and Blood Pressure', *JAMA*, v. 253, pp. 530–4, 1985

46. A. G. Shaper and S. J. Pocock, 'Blood Lead and Blood Pressure', *British Medical Journal*, v. 291, pp. 1147–9, 1985

47. J. N. Candy, et al., 'Aluminosilicates and Senile Plaque For-

mation in Alzheimer's Disease', *Lancet*, pp. 354–7, 15 February 1986

48. T. H. Maugh, 'Acid Rain's Effects on People Assessed', *Science*, v. 226, pp. 1408–10, 1984

49. Parliamentary Reply, Hansard, House of Commons, 10 June 1985

4 *The Strange Death of Europe's Trees*

1. E.g., B. Ulrich, 'Interaction of Indirect and Direct Effects of Air Pollution in Forests, Air Pollution and Plants: Proceedings of the Second European Conference on Chemistry and the Environment in May 1984', VCH Verlagsgesellschaft, Weinheim, 1985

2. E.g., B. Prinz, et al., 'Responses of German Forests in Recent Years: Cause for Concern Elsewhere? Effects of Acidic Deposition on Forests, Wetlands and Agricultural Ecosystems, (Proceedings of NATO advanced research workshop on acid rain organized by NATO, in Toronto, Canada, May 1986)', Springer Verlag, Berlin (in press)

3. E.g., M. Ashmore, et al., 'The Role of Ozone in Forest Damage in West Germany', *Ambio*, v. 14, pp. 81–7, 1985

4. N. van Breemen, et al., 'Soil Acidification from Atmospheric Ammonium Sulphate in Forest Canopy Throughfall', *Nature*, v. 299, pp. 548–50, 1982

5. B. Nihlgard, 'The Ammonium Hypothesis – an Additional Explanation to the Forest Dieback in Europe', *Ambio*, v. 14, pp. 2–8, 1985

6. G. Abrahamsen and B. Tveite, 'Effects of Air Pollution on Forest and Forest Growth', Paper to Stockholm Conference on the Acidification of the Environment, 1982

7. G. Abrahamsen, 'Effects of Acidic Deposition on Forest Soil and Vegetation, Ecological Effects of Deposited Sulphur and Nitrogen Compounds', Proceedings of a Royal Society discussion meeting held in September 1983

8. T. Paces, 'The pH and Concentrations of Sulphate Nitrate and Aluminium in the Run-off from Representative Catchments in the Elbe River Basin', Paper to Stockholm Conference on Acidification of the Environment, 1982

9. P. Greenfelt and H. Hultberg, 'Effects of Nitrogen Deposition on the Acidification of Terrestrial and Aquatic Ecosystems', *Water Air and Soil Pollution*, 1986

10. D. MacKenzie, 'Acid Rain May Trigger Avalanches', *New Scientist*, p. 10, 2 January 1986

11. 1985 Forest Damage Survey, West German Federal Ministry of Food, Agriculture and Forestry

12. Forestry Research 1985, Forestry Commission

13. D. Redfern, during discussions recorded in the Proceedings of Acid Rain Inquiry held in Edinburgh in 1984 under the auspices of the Scottish Wildlife Trust

14. C. Rose and M. Neville, 'Final Report: Tree Dieback Survey', Friends of the Earth, 1985

15. Forestry Commission Research and Development Paper 142: 'Forest Health and Air Pollution: 1984 Survey'

16. F. Pearce, 'Foresters "Can't See the Dead Wood for the Trees"', *New Scientist*, p. 20, 7 November 1985

17. F. Last, 'Direct Effects of Air Pollutants, Single and in Mixtures, on Plants and Plant Assemblages', Proceedings of Symposium on Acid Deposition: A Challenge for Europe, Commission of the European Communities, Karlsruhe, September 1983

18. M. Ashmore, 'Effects of Ozone on Vegetation in the United Kingdom', Proceedings of an International Workshop on the Evaluation and Assessment of the Effects of Photochemical Oxidants in March 1984, Goteborg, Swedish Environment Research Institute

19. M. Ashmore and C. Dalpra, 'Effects of London's Air on Plant Growth', *London Environmental Bulletin*, Scientific Services Branch, Greater London Council, Autumn 1985

20. M. Ashmore, et al., 'A Survey of Ozone Levels in the British Isles Using Indicator Plants', *Nature*, v. 276, pp. 813–15, 1978

21. T. A. Mansfield and P. H. Freer-Smith, 'Effects of Urban Air Pollution on Plant Growth', *Biology Review*, v. 56, pp. 343–68, 1981

22. G. P. Dohmen, et al., 'Air Pollution Increases Aphis Fabae Pest Potential', *Nature*, v. 307, pp. 52–3, 1984

23. G. P. Dohmen, 'Secondary Effects of Air Pollution: Enhanced Aphid Growth', *Environmental Pollution (Series A)*, v. 39, pp. 227–34, 1985

24. *The Times*, 5 July 1976

5 *In the Clouds*

1. A. J. Apling, et al., 'Ozone Concentrations in Southeast England During the Summer of 1976', *Nature*, v. 269, pp. 569–73, 1977

2. R. A. Cox, et al., 'Long-Range Transport of Photochemical Ozone in Northwest Europe', *Nature*, v. 255, pp. 118–21, 1975

3. I. S. Fletcher, 'Ozone Production Downwind of a Large Conurbation', Central Electricity Generating Board Technology Planning and Research Division, September 1985

4. R. G. Derwent and O. Hov, 'Computer Modelling Studies of Photochemical Air Pollution in North West Europe', UK Atomic Energy Authority Harwell, 1979

5. O. Hov, 'Ozone in the Troposphere: High Level Pollution', *Ambio*, v. 13, pp. 73–9, 1984

6. A. T. Cocks, et al., 'Dispersion Limitations of Oxidation in Power Plant Plumes During Long-Range Transport', *Nature*, v. 305, pp. 122–3, 1983

7. M. Wainwright, et al., 'Effect of Acid Rain on the Solubility of Heavy Metal Oxides and Fluorspar Added to Soil', *The Science of the Total Environment*, v. 23, pp. 85–90, 1982

8. W. J. McElroy, 'Sources of Hydrogen Peroxide in Cloudwater: Implications for the Oxidation of Tropospheric SO_2', Central Electricity Generating Board Technology Planning and Research Division, April 1985

9. S. A. Penkett, 'Hydrogen Peroxide in Cloudwater', *Nature*, v. 319, p. 624, 1986

10. B. E. A. Fisher and P. A. Clark, 'Testing a Statistical Long-Range Transport Model on European and North American Observations', later published in *Air Pollution Modelling and its Application IV*, ed. C. de Wispelaere, Plenum, New York, 1985

11. D. Fowler and J. N. Cape, Presentation to Meeting of Scottish Wildlife Trust, September 1984

12. G. P. Gervat, 'Clouds at Ground Level: Samples from the Southern Pennines', Central Electricity Generating Board Technology Planning and Research Division, February 1985

13. K. C. Weathers, et al., 'A Regional Acidic Cloud/Fog Water Event in the Eastern U S', *Nature*, v. 319, pp. 657–8, 1986

14. B. Hileman, 'Acid Fog', *Environmental Science and Technology*, v. 17, pp. 117A–120A, 1983

6 Smoke-Filled Rooms

1. Committee on Air Pollution, Cmnd 9322, November 1954
2. W. S. Kyte, 'Some Implications of Possible Emission Control Technologies in the Electric Power Industry', Paper to Conference on Controls of Acid Emissions in the UK, organized by the Institution of Chemical Engineers, November 1985
3. Evidence from Industrial Air Pollution Inspectorate to House of Commons Environment Committee Inquiry into Acid Rain, 1984
4. F. Pearce, 'Science and Politics Don't Mix at Acid Rain Debate', New Scientist, p. 3, 1 July 1982
5. P. F. Chester, 'Alternatives to Flue Gas Desulphurization', Central Electricity Generating Board, October 1985
6. N. Schofield, 'The Cost of Various Alternatives for Reducing Emissions of Sulphur Dioxide', Paper presented by the Department of the Environment 'in confidence' to the Clean Air Council, c. 1979
7. Minister for Environment, Norway, Published as Appendix 3 to Follow-up to the Environment Committee Report on Acid Rain, House of Commons Environment Committee, November 1985
8. M. Benarie, 'Overall Economic Aspects of Various Abatement Strategies and of the Processes for Reduction of Emissions', Symposium on Acid Deposition: A Challenge for Europe, Commission of the European Communities, Karlsruhe, September 1983
9. T. W. Waddell, 'The Economic Damages of Air Pollution', US Environmental Protection Agency, 1974
10. New Scientist, p. 21, 14 November 1985
11. R. F. Wright and A. Henriksen, 'Restoration of Norwegian Lakes by Reduction in Sulphur Deposition', Nature, v. 305, pp. 422–4, 1983
12. N. Christopherson and H. M. Seip, 'Mechanisms and Prognosis of Freshwater Acidification: A Modelling Approach', Paper to Stockholm Conference on Acidification of the Environment, 1982
13. M. Holdgate, 'Concluding Remarks', Ecological Effects of Deposited Sulphur and Nitrogen Compounds, Proceedings of Royal Society Discussion Meeting, September 1983

Index